Reading and the Mental Lexicon

Marcus Taft

School of Psychology
University of New South Wales
Australia

LAWRENCE ERLBAUM ASSOCIATES, PUBLISHERS
Hove and London (UK)   Hillsdale (USA)

Reprinted in paperback, 1993

Lawrence Erlbaum Associates Ltd., Publishers
27 Palmeira Mansions
Church Road
Hove
East Sussex, BN3 2FA
UK

100 1672614

British Library Cataloguing in Publication Data

Taft, Marcus
   Reading and the mental lexicon
   I. Title
   1. Reading. Psychology
   428.4019

   ISBN 0-86377-110-6 (Hbk)
   ISBN 0-86377-335-4 (Pbk)

Printed and bound by BPCC Wheatons Ltd., Exeter

*I dedicate this book to the thousands of
subjects who have willingly exposed their
lexicons in the cause of science*

Contents

Preface

In early 1985 I had the following idea. The topic of lexical access has been heavily researched and debated in recent years, yet no book exists focusing solely on that topic. Instead of remediating this situation by writing a book centred around my own idiosyncratic approach, I thought I would involve several prominent cognitive psychologists who could provide a range of different theoretical approaches to the issues. What I planned was to ask each of these people a series of questions about a variety of topics in lexical processing, and then I would contribute an overview for each question. I am very grateful to Curtis Becker, Max Coltheart, Ken Forster, John Morton, and Mark Seidenberg for agreeing to participate in this venture. Unfortunately, it soon became clear to all of us that the task I had set was an unrealistically onerous one, and after a year with nothing forthcoming, I came to the inevitable conclusion that I would have to stop passing the buck and would either have to take on the task myself or ditch the whole enterprise. Since it seemed a pity that there were no books written on the topic of lexical processing, I decided to take the former approach, and despite the many occasions when I was sorry that I hadn't taken the latter approach, the task is at last completed.

While the orientation I have adopted will inevitably be idiosyncratic, I hope that I have been able satisfactorily to analyse a range of different approaches to the topic. In fact, my own thinking about lexical processing has evolved quite considerably as a result of having to seriously evaluate the empirical and theoretical literature. For those who know my previous standpoint on lexical access, particularly in the domain of morphological processing, the theoretical framework I end up using in this volume might come as a surprise. It also might come as a disappointment, since my new position is more flexible and less specified than my old position, and therefore more difficult to falsify. A move in such a direction, however, is the inevitable result of advocating a strong and falsifiable view and having others demonstrate problems with it. Nevertheless, the old position still remains in the literature as a testable alternative.

A word should be said about the scope of the book's review of lexical processing. In order to keep the book within the prescribed word limit, it was necessary to have a fairly narrow focus. The main body of research that is examined involves empirical studies where normal adults make some sort of identification response to visually presented letter strings. Hence, developmental research is eschewed. So too, for the most part, is neuropsychological evidence. Given that a number of books have been written about dysfunctions of lexical processing (e.g. M. Coltheart, Patterson, & Marshall, 1980; Ellis, 1988; Patterson, Marshall, & M. Coltheart, 1985), there are very few that provide an overview of normal adult lexical processing (however, see sections in Henderson, 1982; Mitchell, 1982, and also the introductory coverage by Aitchison, 1987), I decided to apply the limited number of words at my disposal to this latter issue. In addition, I decided that the body of research on eye movements in reading, while clearly relevant, tends to address questions that are different to those of concern here. Again, passing reference is made to such studies, but the interested reader is referred to other books that cover this research area far more thoroughly (e.g. Just & Carpenter, 1987; Rayner, 1983, 1989). The lexical processing of spoken words was also overlooked (hence the title of this book), since it too is a major area that warrants a book unto itself (see for example, Frauenfelder & Tyler, 1987).

What I do cover is the following: Chapter 1 provides a description of the basic models of lexical processing and the basic empirical findings, while in Chapter 2 we see how the models account for the findings. A discussion of how the semantic and syntactic characteristics of a word influence lexical processing, both in and out of its sentential context, is found in Chapter 3. Chapter 4 presents an account of the involvement of phonology in visual lexical processing. It is in this chapter that a new model is developed. In Chapter 5, I pursue the question of whether the morphological and/or syllabic structure of a word influences processing. The final chapter provides an overview and a brief discussion of what are likely to be major areas of interest in the near future, namely, the distributed network approach and cross-linguistic studies.

It should be said that the distributed network approach has already aroused considerable interest and controversy in the field. I have not, however, incorporated it into the main body of the book. This is partly because the model was introduced into the literature at a late stage of writing, and partly because it was unclear to me how its inclusion would illuminate the issues that are discussed.

Finally, I would like to thank David Cottrell, Sally Andrews, and Ken Forster for the advice and encouragement that they have afforded me at various stages of writing, and would also like to acknowledge the technical help provided by Bruce Russell, Kim Ter Horst, and Fay Sudweeks.

Support provided by the Australian Research Council during the course of writing this book is gratefully acknowledged.

M.T.
Sydney
January 1991

CHAPTER ONE

Introduction

"Even with hard yakka, you've got Buckley's of understanding this dinkum English sentence, unless you're an Aussie."[1]

An Australian has no difficulty comprehending the above sentence, while other English speakers might struggle. The words "yakka", "Buckley's", and "dinkum" are in the vocabulary of most Australians, that is, they are stored as entries in the mental lexicon, and therefore an Australian has access to the meanings of these words and can consequently comprehend the sentence. If one possessed no mental lexicon, communication through language would be precluded. It is therefore important to address the question about how lexical information is stored and how it is retrieved. This is the issue of lexical access.

The most rudimentary assumption that we can begin with is that lexical information about a word becomes available when some encoded sensory version of the incoming physical stimulus is found to be congruent with a word encoded in lexical memory. The issues that have been examined in the area of lexical processing concern the way in which this sensory-to-lexical match occurs, the code in which the match occurs, and also the nature of the information that becomes available once a lexical entry is accessed. These questions relate to the issues of how we read, how we understand spoken language, how we speak, and how we spell. Most of the research that has been conducted in the area of lexical access, however, has centred upon visual word recognition, that is, lexical access in reading, and it is this aspect of lexical processing that will be the focus of the present monograph.

Obviously, one of the most important characteristics of a word is its meaning, and it is indeed one of the most important aims of the lexical access process to make the meaning of the word available to the sentence comprehension system. Once the lexical entry for a word is accessed, the semantic properties of that word become available (as well as the syntactic properties, spelling, and pronunciation). The way in which the semantic properties of words are represented and organized, however, will not be considered in any great detail in this volume. Instead, the focus will be upon the structural characteristics of words, since it is these that are crucial in the accessing of lexical entries. It is possible though, that the semantic context in which a word occurs might influence lexical access to that word, and so discussion of this issue is clearly germane to any examination of the nature of lexical access. This aspect of semantic processing will be taken up in a later chapter.

MODELS OF LEXICAL ACCESS

Various different approaches have been adopted in attempting to model the processes involved in lexical access. I will begin by outlining the basic framework of the most influential of these models, and will then, in the next chapter, elaborate upon this by describing how the models go about explaining a number of important experimental findings.

The Search Model

This model of lexical access says that the lexicon is serially scanned until a match is found between the incoming sensory information and a lexical entry. Inspired by the work of H. Rubenstein (H. Rubenstein, Garfield, & Millikan, 1970; H. Rubenstein, Lewis, & M.A. Rubenstein, 1971a, b), the main proponent of this approach has been Forster and his colleagues (e.g. Forster, 1976, 1989; Forster & Bednall, 1976; Forster & Davis, 1984; O'Connor & Forster, 1981; Taft & Forster, 1975, 1976).

Since it is very unlikely that the complete list of known words is searched every time a word is to be processed, Forster suggests that each search is confined to a particular subset of lexical entries, termed a "bin". Bins are defined on the basis of sensory characteristics (e.g. "all words beginning with s and ending in e") and are selected prior to the initiation of the search procedure.

In order to explain how a sensory-to-lexical match can be made when the sensory input is visual as well as when it is auditory, the search model includes one set of lexical representations that are compatible with orthographic information (i.e. the visual form of the word) and another which is compatible with phonological information (i.e. the auditory form of the word). Both of these sets of representations, called the orthographic access file and the phonological access file respectively, feed into the modality free lexicon proper or "master file" where the full information about a word is available (i.e. its meaning, part of speech, spelling, etc.). The architecture of the search model is depicted in Fig.1.1.

The orthographic access file is serially searched when a letter string is visually presented, and when a lexical representation is found to adequately match with the encoded sensory input, this directly leads to the corresponding master file entry. The full spelling of this word can

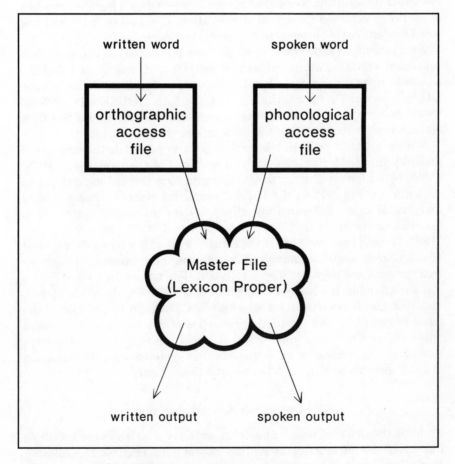

FIG. 1.1. A simplified version of the search framework.

then be checked back to the original stimulus (or the representation of this stimulus in working memory) and if it matches, the letter string can then be recognized as being that word. If it does not match, the search resumes in the orthographic access file in order to find a more suitable match.

The Logogen Model

An alternative account of lexical access mechanisms is a model incorporating the notion of activation, the first example of which was the logogen model put forward by Morton (1969, 1970). Each lexical entry is seen as an evidence collecting device or "logogen" which becomes increasingly activated the more the features of the incoming stimulus resemble those of the word that it represents. Once a logogen reaches some predetermined threshold of activation, it is said to "fire" and the word consequently becomes available for response.

As an example, if the word HOUSE were presented, all logogens that represent words beginning with the letter H would be activated slightly, as would all words ending in E, all five letter words, all words containing OU, and so on. Therefore, the logogens for both HOUSE and HORSE would be activated. However, the logogen for HOUSE would fire first since it is activated by all of the incoming sensory features.

While it would be feasible for logogens to accept both visual and auditory input, Morton has, in later versions of the model (e.g. 1979, 1982), opted for separate orthographic and phonological logogen input systems (see Fig. 1.2) on the basis of empirical evidence that auditory and visual input differentially affect the lexical access system (e.g. Winnick & Daniel, 1970; Warren & Morton, 1982; Clarke & Morton, 1983). Thus the architecture of the logogen system is very similar to that of the search model, although of course the mechanism by which an entry is accessed is quite different. In addition, where the search model has a master file, the logogen model has a "cognitive system" along with visual and auditory output logogen systems. The cognitive system is the locus of semantic and syntactic properties of words, while the visual output system provides word spellings, and the auditory output system provides pronunciations. How these output systems actually make use of a logogen mechanism is, however, not made clear.

The Interactive-Activation Model

Perhaps the most influential model of word recognition in recent times has been the interactive-activation model proposed by McClelland, Rumelhart, and colleagues (e.g. Glushko, 1979; McClelland, 1987;

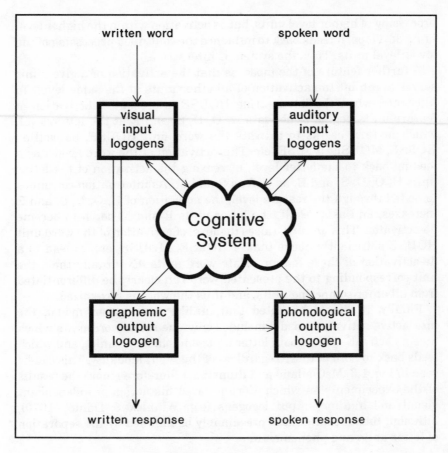

FIG. 1.2. A simplified version of the logogen framework.

McClelland & Elman, 1986; McClelland & Rumelhart, 1981; Rumelhart & McClelland, 1982). While not originally put forward as a model of lexical access, such a label is certainly appropriate since the model attempts to explain what goes on between the input of a verbal stimulus and the output of a recognition response to that stimulus.

The interactive-activation framework is an elaboration on the logogen approach, involving sets of processing units that behave in a somewhat similar way to logogens. These sets correspond to higher and higher levels of language structure, for example, visual feature units, letter units, and word units (see Fig. 1.3). When a word is visually presented, the appropriate visual feature units are activated, which in turn activate appropriate letter units, which similarly activate word units. Not only does the activation of lower level units influence the processing of higher level units, but as activation within the higher level units develops, it feeds back to influence the continued processing of the lower level units. Thus the system is interactive.

A further feature of the model is that the activation of a given unit serves to inhibit the activation of all other units at the same level. To illustrate, when the letter string HOUSE is presented, activation of feature units begins to activate H, O, U, S, and E at the letter level, which in turn begins to activate the word unit HOUSE, as well as HORSE, MOUSE, ROUSE, etc. This activation at the word level starts feeding back to the letter level, increasing the activation of the letter units H, O, U, S, and E, as well as R and M. As information continues to be fed through the feature level, the activation of H, O, U, S, and E increases, and as a result, the letter units R and M begin to become de-activated. This, in turn, raises the level of activation of the word unit HOUSE sufficiently above that of HORSE, MOUSE, etc. to lead to a de-activation of these inappropriate word units. Eventually then, the unit corresponding to the presented word can clearly be differentiated from all other competing units, and thus the word is recognized.

Finally, it should be noted that, unlike the logogen model, the interactive-activation model includes only one set of word units which accepts activation from both letter units and phoneme units, and which feeds back to both of these regardless of the input modality. This can be seen in Fig. 1.3. McClelland and Rumelhart therefore ignore the results of the experiments on which Morton based his notion of independent visual and auditory input logogens (e.g. Winnick & Daniel, 1970), although these results could presumably be handled by the separation of letter units and phoneme units.

The Verification Model

The output of the interactive-activation model is a single word that has been isolated from a set of active candidates by means of an inhibitory mechanism working on competing units. The verification model provides a different method by which a single word can be selected from a set of active candidates.

According to the "verification" model (e.g. Becker, 1976; Becker & Killion, 1977) or "activation-verification" model (e.g. Paap, McDonald, Schvaneveldt, & Noel, 1987; Paap, Newsome, McDonald, & Schvaneveldt, 1982), the logogen system generates a set of candidates rather than a single output. This set of candidates is then sequentially checked back against the sensory representation of the stimulus (as stored in visual memory), until a match is made. For example, when HOUSE is presented, the lexical entries for HORSE,

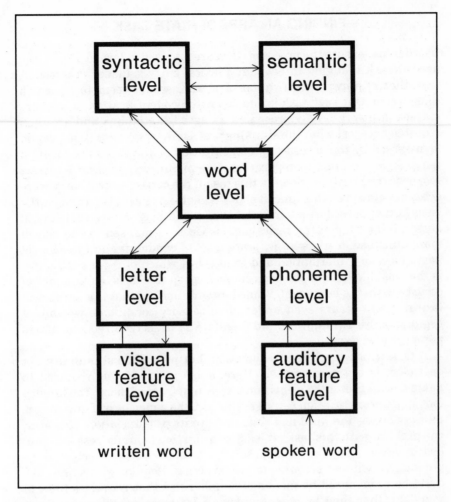

FIG. 1.3. A simplified version of the interactive-activation framework.

MOUSE, and ROUSE might be activated sufficiently for those words to enter the candidate set along with HOUSE, but at the subsequent verification stage, the latter is selected ahead of the other candidates when it is established that it correctly checks back to the presented letter string.

These then are the four major models of lexical processing which we will now examine in terms of how they stand up to empirical scrutiny. Before discussing what the empirical findings are, however, let us first examine the question of how lexical processing is actually measured.

FINDING AN APPROPRIATE TASK

In order to measure the processes that are involved in lexical access, one needs a task that guarantees that a lexical entry is indeed accessed. A task that requires identification of a word would seem to be worth considering. One such task is a tachistoscopic identification task where subjects are very briefly presented a degraded stimulus and are then required to report what the stimulus was. Difficulty of processing would be assessed by the accuracy of identification or the exposure duration required for accurate identification. One might consider that a correct response could only be given in this task if the correct lexical entry were accessed. However, it is conceivable that subjects guess the word on the basis of partial information only. While guessing does entail lexical access, it does not entail lexical access via a normal sensory-to-lexical match. Instead, one might generate a set of candidates on the basis of partial sensory information and then select which of these candidates is the most likely to be the correct one (e.g. on the basis of frequency of occurrence in the language). While it might turn out that this is the way lexical access occurs even under ideal sensory conditions, we cannot begin with this assumption, and therefore a task is required which uses non-degraded stimuli.

A task which involves identification, but where the stimuli are not degraded, is the naming task. Here, subjects are simply required to name a word presented clearly on a screen in front of them. The latency to initiate pronunciation can be assumed to be a measure of how long it takes to access the word and thus retrieve its pronunciation. However, one problem with this task, at least as a starting point for research into lexical access, is that it is possible for many letter strings to be pronounced without recourse to lexical access. Regular words like CAT could be pronounced by means of simple rules that convert letters to sounds, rather than by means of lexical information. Whether or not words are actually pronounced by means of rules is something that will be discussed later, but for a starting point where lexical access is inarguably required, we need to find a different task.

The task that has been most frequently adopted in the study of lexical access has been the lexical decision task. Pioneered by H. Rubenstein and colleagues (e.g. H. Rubenstein et al., 1970, 1971a, b), this task has proven to be a fruitful method for exploring the nature of the mental lexicon. In a lexical decision experiment, subjects are required to discriminate words from nonwords by pressing one button if the presented stimulus is a word and another button if it is not. Speed and accuracy of response are used to measure the difficulty of lexical processing. As long as the nonwords are possible English constructions (i.e. they are stimuli like FLINK rather than LKFNI), the task can only be performed by ascertaining whether the letter string is stored in the lexicon or not. For example, the letter string DINKUM would be classified by most English speakers as a nonword, but an Australian would classify it as a word because it has a lexical entry. There is no basis on which to classify DINKUM as a nonword other than on the fact that it is not lexically stored.

The lexical decision task, therefore, looks like a promising place to begin the quest for an understanding of the processes involved in lexical access. Of course, one does not want to rely solely on a single task in developing one's account of lexical processing since there may be special strategies associated with that task (see the last section of Chapter 2). Therefore, one would ultimately like to see one's account supported by findings from more than one task.

There are several basic findings that are consistently obtained using the visual lexical decision task and these must be explained by any model which purports to be an account of lexical access. While there are, of course, many other effects observed using lexical decision and other tasks (which will be described later), the following are perhaps the most fundamental in that something is probably amiss with any experiment where these effects are tested, but not observed.

BASIC LEXICAL DECISION FINDINGS

1. *Frequency effect.* The time taken to make a lexical decision response to a word of high frequency in the language is less than that to a word of low frequency in the language (e.g. Forster & Chambers, 1973; H. Rubenstein et al., 1970; Taft, 1979a; Whaley, 1978). For example, subjects will recognize the common word HOUSE more quickly on average than the rarer word ROUSE.

2. *Lexical status effect.* Response times are longer when classifying a letter string as a nonword than when classifying a letter string as a word (e.g. H. Rubenstein et al., 1970). That is, subjects take longer on average to say that FLINK is not a word than to say that BLINK is.

3. *Nonword legality effect.* Lexical decision times to nonwords like FLINK, which have a legal orthographic structure, are slower than to random letter strings like LFKNI (e.g. H. Rubenstein et al., 1971a; Stanners, Forbach, & Headley, 1971; Stanners & Forbach, 1973).

4. *Word similarity effect.* When a legal nonword is sufficiently similar to a word, it is difficult to classify as a nonword. For example, a nonword like TRIAN, which is a word with two letters transposed, is associated with longer response times and a higher error rate than a nonword like TRUAN which is not generated from a word in this way

(e.g. Chambers, 1979; O'Connor & Forster, 1981). M. Coltheart, Davelaar, Jonasson, and Besner (1977) demonstrated what they called a "neighbourhood size effect" whereby the more words that a nonword was one letter different to, the longer was the response time. For example, the neighbourhood of JATE includes GATE, HATE, RATE, DATE, JUTE, JADE, etc. while the neighbourhood of RALP only includes RAMP and RASP, and therefore the former takes longer to respond to than the latter.

5. *Repetition priming effect.* Response latencies to a word are reduced when presented for a second time, so that, for example, CAMEL is classified more quickly when it has been preceded by CAMEL than when it has not (e.g. Forbach, Stanners, & Hochhaus, 1974; Kirsner & Smith, 1974; D.L. Scarborough, Cortese, & H.S. Scarborough, 1977).

6. *Semantic priming effect.* When a word is preceded by a semantically related word, it becomes easier to classify as a word (e.g. Meyer & Schvaneveldt, 1971). Latencies to recognize CAT, for example, are shorter if it is preceded by DOG than if it is preceded by SIX.

7. *Visual degradation effect.* When a letter string is visually degraded, it becomes more difficult to classify as a word or nonword. There are a number of ways in which a word can be degraded. For example, the word might be presented with a covering pattern of dots (e.g. Meyer, Schvaneveldt, & Ruddy, 1974; Stanners, Jastrzembski, & Westbrook, 1975), the intensity of the stimulus might be reduced (e.g. Becker & Killion, 1977), or the letters making up the word might be of alternating case, as with aPpLe (e.g. Besner, 1983). While the visual degradation effect is neither surprising nor interesting in itself, we will see that it becomes important when we consider how it interacts with some of the other effects.

How then do the models account for these seven basic effects?

NOTE

1. The sentence means: "Even with hard work, you've got no chance of understanding this genuine English sentence, unless you're Australian".

CHAPTER TWO

Evaluation of Models

In this chapter we will examine the way in which the four types of lexical access models account for the basic effects observed in visual lexical decision tasks. Later in the chapter, however, we will consider whether the lexical decision task is indeed the most appropriate basis on which to evaluate the models.

THE FREQUENCY EFFECT

According to the serial search account, words are stored within a bin in order of frequency so that high frequency words are simply accessed prior to low frequency words, and can therefore be verified against the original stimulus earlier. Hence, high frequency words will be responded to more rapidly than low frequency words.

The verification model accounts for the frequency effect at the post-access verification stage rather than during the accessing of the lexical candidates. Once the candidates are activated, the sequence of verification is based upon word frequency. Such a notion requires information about word frequency to be represented in each lexical entry, with that information being used to check higher frequency words back to the original stimulus before lower frequency words.

Therefore, both the search model and the verification model explain frequency effects in terms of serial processing. In both models, verification occurs for high frequency words before low frequency words, but this is instantiated differently in the two models. In the search model, frequency effects arise from the access process itself. If the first accessed entry does not acceptably check with the original stimulus, then a second, necessarily lower frequency candidate is tried out, and so on. In the verification model, on the other hand, the development of the candidate set is not affected by frequency and instead, information about frequency which is associated with the accessed candidates, guides the order of verification.

If it is the case that frequency effects arise at the verification stage, then it follows that such effects should be eliminated if the verification stage is eliminated (Paap et al., 1982). A series of lexical decision experiments carried out by Dobbs, Friedman, and Lloyd (1985) attempted to do this by using very brief or masked presentations, the rationale being that such a presentation style would eliminate the perceptual trace of the stimulus and thus preclude verification. Their failure to eliminate the frequency effect under these conditions was taken to be evidence against the verification model. However, if this experimental technique had actually succeeded in preventing verification, then according to the verification model, subjects could not have made a lexical decision response at all since the word/nonword discrimination is made at the verification stage. Therefore, the interpretation of experiments using this approach is thrown into doubt.

Frequency effects are explained by the logogen model in terms of the differential time taken for the threshold to be reached. One can either say that high frequency words have a lower activation threshold than low frequency words, or that they have a higher initial "resting level" of activation; these seem to amount to much the same thing. Either way, the logogen for a low frequency word will require the input of more sensory information in order to fire than will a high frequency word and thus will take longer to reach threshold.

Being an activation model, the interactive-activation model can also explain the frequency effect in terms of the resting activation of a unit being influenced by word frequency. Another way of representing this notion in the interactive-activation framework is to say that more frequently used connections between units provide stronger activation than less frequently used connections. For example, it is more often the case when the letter H occurs in a letter string, that the letter string is the word HOUSE than it is the word HOUND and, therefore, the strength of the connection between the letter unit H and the word unit HOUSE will be greater than between the letter unit H and the word unit HOUND.

THE LEXICAL STATUS EFFECT

The serial search model has no difficulty in explaining the lexical status effect. A nonword takes longer to respond to than a word because the former requires an exhaustive search to determine that there is no appropriate lexical entry, while the search for the latter terminates when a lexical match is achieved (i.e. the search is "self-terminating"). Therefore a lexical decision about a word occurs earlier than a lexical decision about a nonword.

When attempting to account for the lexical status effect in terms of the logogen model, one immediately confronts the issue of how a nonword response is made at all.[1] If the system is waiting for a logogen to reach threshold, at what point does it decide that no logogen is ever going to reach threshold, thus implying that the item is not a word? What has been proposed in answer to this question is simply that there is a deadline after which a nonword classification is made if no logogen has reached threshold (M. Coltheart et al., 1977). With this minor modification, it is clear that nonword responses will take longer to make than word responses, since the latter will arise from processes occurring prior to the deadline.

Although it involves a similar access mechanism to the logogen model, the interactive-activation account does not so readily explain how a nonword response can be made. This is because the decision about which is the most appropriate word unit is determined by relative activation rather than absolute activation. That is, a unit is selected when it becomes activated to a criterially greater degree than any other unit, not when it becomes activated to some predetermined level. What one needs to suggest then, is that a nonword response is made when no unit develops sufficiently greater activation than any other unit before some deadline is reached. But there are potential problems with this.

In particular, it seems to be possible for a nonword that is similar to a word to activate a single unit beyond any other yet still be classifiable as a nonword. For example, the letter string KONDERGARTEN is clearly not a word, yet the unit that stands for KINDERGARTEN will surely at some stage be activated well above any other units given that 11 of the 12 letters overlap. More will be said about this in relation to word similarity effects, but suffice it to say at this point, that the interactive-activation model cannot simply explain how the straightforward task of discriminating a nonword from a word is carried out.

Finally, the verification model provides two loci for making nonword responses. First, it may be the case that the presented nonword is not sufficiently similar to any words for there to be a candidate set at all; and secondly, if a candidate set is actually generated, the nonword classification response can be made when all of the candidates fail the verification test. The lexical status effect will be obtained in the second case since the verification phase will be exhaustive for nonwords and self-terminating for words. However, in the first case, the comparison of nonword to word responses is less predictable since it depends on how long the system is prepared to wait until it decides that no words are going to enter the candidate set. It is at this first stage that the verification model is able to account for the nonword legality effect, since illegal nonwords (e.g. LKFNI) will not generate a candidate set, while legal ones (e.g. FLINK) will.

How do the other models explain the legality effect?

THE NONWORD LEGALITY EFFECT

The search model could say that the illegal string fails to find an appropriate bin and that it therefore never enters into the search stage. However, this explanation is not very convincing in the light of a study by Novik (1974) which demonstrated a "lexical" effect on nonword classification responses to illegal strings, namely, that meaningful strings like FBI were responded to more slowly than meaningless strings like BFI. Instead, the search model needs to give an account similar to that given by the verification model, namely, that illegal strings fail to match with any lexical entries, whereas legal strings do provide sufficient lexical matches for at least some lexical representations to enter the checking stage.

For the logogen model and the interactive-activation model to explain orthographic legality effects, they need to modify their deadline notion. The period that elapses before a nonword decision is made cannot simply be measured from the time that the stimulus is presented, or otherwise all nonwords would be responded to in the same amount of time.

Morton proposes that for a logogen to have sufficient strength to reach threshold, it is not just the amount of activation that is taken into account, but the amount of activation relative to other activity in the logogen system. One way of instantiating this so that nonword responses can be explained is to say that the threshold level for all logogens is influenced by the amount of overall activity within the logogen system. The deadline for deciding that no suitable entry has been accessed is also influenced by the amount of activity in the system (M.Coltheart et al., 1977) since the more activity there is, the greater the likelihood that a logogen will ultimately reach threshold and therefore, the longer it is worth waiting for this to happen. Since orthographically illegal nonwords arouse little activity in the logogen system, the deadline will be reached relatively early compared to orthographically legal nonwords, and thus the legality effect will be observed. The idea of flexible deadlines will be discussed further in the light of word similarity effects.

THE WORD SIMILARITY EFFECT

The delay in responding to nonwords that are similar to words is explained by the search model via its reiterative post-access checking procedure. For example, the stimulus TRIAN is sufficiently similar to the lexical entry TRAIN for the latter to be accessed by the former. If the error is not picked up at the checking stage, then the stimulus will be incorrectly classified as a word. If the error is noticed, the search will continue until the end of the search space. In the case of TRUAN the search will be exhaustive without any such interruption and thus the stimulus will be more rapidly classifiable as a nonword.

One might ask why the nonword classification cannot be made immediately at the point when the checking process has revealed a mismatch, without resuming the serial search. The answer to this is that, if the response were made at this point, any word that resembled a higher frequency word would never be recognized. For example, the low frequency word MINUET would be mistakenly classified as a nonword once the lexical entry for the higher frequency word MINUTE was accessed and then found to be inappropriate. Only if there were a further search would the lexical entry for MINUET be located.

The above idea leads to a prediction about lexical decision responses to words like MINUET which are similar to other words. Since the higher frequency similar word will interrupt the search for the lower frequency word, one would expect to observe a "word similarity" effect on low frequency words just as one does for nonwords. That is, MINUET should take longer to recognize than a word of the same frequency which is not so similar to another word (e.g. BEAGLE). Chambers (1979) has in fact presented evidence in support of this hypothesis, as has Grainger, O'Regan, Jacobs, and Segui (1989) using letter substitution (e.g. POLITE receives interference from POLICE). What these investigators did not test, however, were high frequency words that were similar to low frequency words. According to the search model, for example, response times to MINUTE should be unaffected by the existence of the word MINUET since the lexical entry for the latter should never be encountered during the lexical processing of the former. Whether this is true or not remains to be resolved; however, there are several unpublished studies which suggest that high frequency words do receive as much interference from the other word, as low frequency words do

(Andrews, 1987; Kinoshita, 1984; Mitchell, Sharkey, & Fox, 1983). Such a finding, if clearly established, would be very damaging to a frequency ordered serial search model.

The verification model can explain word similarity effects on nonwords quite simply. Nonwords that are similar to real words will create a larger candidate set than those which are not. Since an attempt will be made to verify (unsuccessfully) every candidate in the set, the size of the candidate set should affect classification times.

As far as responses to words like MINUET and MINUTE go, the verification model predicts the same as the search model. Both words will enter the candidate set when either is presented, but when it is the higher frequency word that is presented (MINUTE), successful verification will occur before any attempt is made to verify the lower frequency candidate and thus, the response should not be delayed relative to that made to a word which is not similar to another word. On the other hand, responses to the lower frequency word (MINUET) will be delayed by the verification attempt on the higher frequency word. The verification model therefore would confront the same problems as the search model if it were to be demonstrated that word similarity effects on word items are unaffected by frequency.

Turning now to the logogen model; if the nonword TRIAN is presented, the logogen for TRAIN will become active since the two have so many features in common. Should this activation be sufficient, the logogen for TRAIN will reach threshold and therefore an error in response will be made, that is, the subject will say that TRIAN is the word TRAIN. This explains the word similarity effect on error rates, but does not account for the more common case where a correct response is made and the effect is observed on reaction times. When subjects correctly say that TRIAN is a nonword, their responses are delayed relative to a control nonword like TRUAN.

The explanation for this requires the same assumption that was made when explaining the nonword legality effect, namely, the ability of logogen thresholds to vary depending upon the amount of activity in the logogen system. This variable threshold assumption explains the word similarity effect on response times, since there will be more activity in the logogen system when TRIAN is presented than when TRUAN is presented, even though TRIAN may not provide sufficient sensory input to the TRAIN logogen for it to reach threshold.

The delay in word responses (e.g. to MINUET) is also explained since the activity in the logogen for MINUTE will raise the threshold for response to MINUET. In other words, a more detailed analysis of the sensory input is required for MINUET to reach threshold than will be required of BEAGLE. Note also that by this account the threshold for response to MINUTE will be raised by activity in the logogen for MINUET, and therefore there should be as much a delay in response times to MINUTE as there is to MINUET compared to control words. This is the result which, if true, would be a major stumbling-block for the search model; yet it would be readily handled, indeed predicted, by the logogen model.

The interactive-activation account is again similar to the logogen account except that the threshold is relative rather than absolute. When TRIAN is presented, the letter units T, R, I, A, and N will be activated, which in turn will activate the word unit TRAIN (as well as TRIAL, TRIANGLE, and so on).

From this description, it might seem that TRAIN and TRIAN could not be differentiated since they include the same letters. However, information about letter order is assumed by McClelland and Rumelhart to be encoded in the letter units by means of context-sensitive coding (as suggested by Wickelgren, 1969, see Rumelhart & McClelland, 1986). According to this system, an A which is preceded by an I and followed by an N is different to an A which is preceded by an R and followed by an I (one can be represented as $_IA_N$ and the other as $_RA_I$) and therefore the word unit TRAIN will not be activated by the letter string TRIAN to the same degree that it would be activated by the letter string TRAIN. In addition, since the unit $_AI_N$ in the word TRAIN has more features in common with the unit $_RI_A$ in TRIAN than it has with the unit $_RU_A$ in TRUAN, it will take longer to accept TRIAN as a nonword than TRUAN.

There are, however, further considerations that confront the interactive-activation position if it is to explain all aspects of the word similarity effect. As the results of Chambers (1979) suggest, responses to nonwords tend to be longer (and less accurate) when two letters have been transposed in a word (e.g. TRIAN) than when a letter has been substituted (e.g. TRAIM). Yet the latter type of nonword has more context-sensitive letter units in common with its source word than the former type does ($_TR$, $_TRA$, and $_RAI$ versus just $_TR$) and therefore it might be thought that letter substitutions should make responding more difficult than letter transpositions.

Furthermore, there are potential problems with the relative threshold notion. As pointed out earlier, the word unit for a long word like KINDERGARTEN should be activated well above any other unit when that word is presented with a substituted letter as in KONDERGARTEN, and thus one might expect the nonword to be always accepted as a word. Yet error rates are actually very low in responding to letter substituted items (Chambers, 1979; Taft, 1987), although reaction times are long. What the interactive-activation account needs in order for the low error rate to be explained is the assumption that inhibition in the letter unit for I is so massive that it outweighs the activation of all the other letters such that the word unit for KINDERGARTEN is not strongly activated above any other word. There cannot, however, be so much inhibition that the response to the item is not delayed.

In sum, the interactive-activation approach would seem to require some complex interaction of activation and inhibition that would account for the lengthy but mostly accurate responses to letter substituted nonwords, as well as the lengthy and quite inaccurate responses to letter transposed nonwords (e.g. O'Connor & Forster, 1981). Such a formulation must be uncontrived enough to be convincing.

It should be pointed out that the only reason why the above problems with an activation-type model are not also ascribed to the logogen model, is that the logogen model is not as detailed in its specification of how the sensory input influences the activation level of logogens. If it were to be more specific, it would presumably run into the same sort of problems as the interactive-activation model does. For example, there needs to be something that prevents the KINDERGARTEN logogen from always reaching threshold when KONDERGARTEN is presented so that an erroneous "word" response is avoided. In fact, since it is obvious to most people that KONDERGARTEN comes from KINDERGARTEN, it seems that the logogen for KINDERGARTEN does reach threshold when KONDERGARTEN is presented.

What this implies is that the erroneous "word" response is suppressed at a stage after the logogen has reached threshold. In other words, the logogen model, and similarly the interactive-activation model, seem to require the existence of a post-access checking stage whereby the orthographic representation of the successfully activated lexical entry is checked against the orthography of the original stimulus, and if it does not match, a nonword response is given.

This checking stage need not necessarily be seen as an integral part of the model, as it is in the verification model, but rather it can be seen as a special strategy that is adopted when nonwords are to be discriminated from words. It should be noted that such a situation does not arise solely in the artificial experimental setting, but also is important for accurate proofreading. When proofreading, one must recognize that a letter string is not a word, and further, one must recover what word it should have been.

There is a final important point regarding word similarity effects that requires comment. A number of studies have demonstrated a word similarity effect on word responses that is facilitatory rather than inhibitory. In particular, it has been shown that the larger the neighbourhood size of a stimulus word (i.e. the more words that are only one letter different to the stimulus word), the faster or more accurate are the responses to that word (Andrews, 1989; McCann & Besner, 1987; Laxon, V. Coltheart, & Keating, 1988). For example, HAND (which is one letter different to SAND, BAND, LAND, HANG, HIND, HARD, etc.) is faster to respond to than HUGE (which is one letter different to only one word, HUGS). Such a result is highly problematical for the search, verification, and logogen models, since these models will always predict interference rather than facilitation arising from access to the wrong word. The interactive-activation model, on the other hand, is able to explain results that are either inhibitory or facilitatory.

During the course of activation in the interactive-activation system, there will be a point when all the words sharing letters with the stimulus word will be feeding activation back down to the letter level and actually increasing the level of activation in the units representing the stimulus word. The increase in activation to the unit representing the stimulus word will have the effect of inhibiting the inappropriate word units. McClelland and Rumelhart (1981) refer to this as the "gang effect". Andrews claims that this gang effect can account for the facilitatory nature of having a large neighbourhood. On the other hand, if the units which represent the words in the neighbourhood are sufficiently activated, they will inhibit the unit representing the stimulus word and this will result in interference. Hence, the interactive-activation model has the luxury of being able to explain both interference and facilitation, should one or the other be observed. While this appears to render the interactive-activation model unfalsifiable, it at least provides an explanation for something which the other models are unable to handle. In Chapter 4, we will look at an alternative way of conceptualizing the neighbourhood size effect within the framework of an interactive-activation system; one which is specific enough to be empirically tested.

THE REPETITION PRIMING EFFECT

The search model has several ways of explaining why a word is responded to more quickly on its second presentation than on its first. One possibility is that a word is moved to the head of the search set after it has been accessed, thus being rapidly accessed on its second presentation. If this were the case, low frequency words would show a larger repetition effect than high frequency words because the improvement to their position in the search space would be greater, and this is what D.L. Scarborough et al. (1977) have demonstrated. However, Forster and Davis (1984) have observed that the interaction between frequency and repetition disappears if the conscious recognition of the first occurrence of the word (i.e. the "prime") is blocked out by a masking procedure, even though the repetition effect itself remains intact.

Forster and Davis conclude from this that a lexical entry is made more accessible by its immediately prior presentation in that the lexical entry has been "opened" and remains open for a short period of time. In addition, repetition effects can arise from a second source which only comes into play when the prime is not masked. This source is episodic memory (see e.g. Tulving, 1972). Forster and Davis suggest that when a prime is not masked it lays down an episodic trace which influences lexical decision responses to the target word. The frequency interaction is claimed to arise from episodic memory, not from lexical memory. They claim that the truly lexical effects of repetition can only be observed using the masked priming technique.

Both the logogen model and the interactive-activation model account for the repetition priming effect by saying that, after a logogen (or unit) has been accessed, its activation level slowly returns toward its resting level. If the word corresponding to this logogen is presented again while there is still residual activation, fewer sensory features will need to be extracted for the logogen to reach threshold again. According to this account, low frequency words should produce a larger repetition effect than high frequency words since the amount of residual activation relative to the resting level of activation will be greater for low frequency words than for high frequency words.

This prediction from the logogen and interactive-activation models, although supported by the results of D.L. Scarborough et al., is not upheld when the prime is masked, given that Forster and Davis found no interaction of frequency and repetition under such conditions. This result, however, could be explained quite naturally by the activation models by saying that, when the sensory representation is eliminated through masking, sensory input into the logogen system ceases. Thus, there is a brief increase in activation in those logogens which have features in common with the prime, but this activation never reaches threshold and therefore no word reaches consciousness. Since the increase in activation would be of the same magnitude regardless of frequency, this accounts for the additive effects of repetition and frequency in the masked priming task. There is, however, a further result that complicates this partial activation account of masked priming.

If all logogens having features in common with the priming stimulus are partly activated prior to being masked, then a prime which is orthographically similar to the target word should lead to a facilitation of response to the target. For example, a masked presentation of the word SAMPLE or the nonword SUMPLE should serve to decrease response times to the target word SIMPLE. It turns out though, that such masked "form priming" only holds true when the target word is similar to few other words (i.e. comes from a small neighbourhood) or when it comes from the same root word as the prime (Forster, Davis, Schoknecht, & Carter, 1987; Forster, 1987). Thus, SAMPLE is primed by SIMPLE since few other words are similar to SAMPLE, and MAKE is primed by MADE since they are morphologically related, but LOOK is not primed by BOOK since it is only one letter different from many other words (e.g. HOOK, COOK, TOOK, LOCK, LOOT, etc.).

Forster (1987) points out that such a pattern of results is difficult to explain by a partial-activation account, since there is no reason for the neighbourhood size of the target to affect the extent of priming, nor for morphologically related words to be treated differently to other words. However, he also acknowledges that the effect of target neighbourhood size is difficult to explain in terms of the search model as well. The sort of assumption that is required by the search model is that there can be a gradation in the amount of "openness" of lexical entries depending on their similarity to the presented word, and this comes very close to saying that "openness" is equivalent to activation.

In addition, there are indications that the effect of a form prime can be inhibitory rather than facilitatory, both when the prime is masked (Forster et al., 1987; Forster, 1987) and when there is no mask (Colombo, 1986; Henderson, Wallis, & Knight, 1984). That is, the prior presentation of BOOK might actually make the recognition of LOOK more difficult. Such a result would seem to be most readily explained by an activation account incorporating inhibitory mechanisms, as in the interactive-activation model. In fact, the inhibitory effects of a form-related prime are extremely difficult, if not impossible, for the search model to explain. Forster concludes that neither the search nor activation approach alone provides a satisfactory explanation for form priming effects.

The verification model explains the basic repetition effect in the same way as the other activation models, since the effect arises at the activation stage. However, the verification model makes a different prediction with regard to the interaction of repetition and frequency. In the logogen and interactive-activation systems, the repetition of a word affects the same mechanisms that are affected by word frequency, and thus repetition and frequency should interact. In the verification system, on the other hand, the two factors affect different parts of the system (i.e. the activation stage is affected by repetition and the verification stage by frequency) and so their effects should be additive. In this way, the verification model can account for the results obtained by Forster and Davis when the prime was masked. However, although the verification model's prediction seems logical, there is a conceptual flaw.

If verification takes place only after a complete set of candidates is established, it is hard to see what the advantage is of having one candidate enter the set faster than it normally would as a result of increased activation due to repetition. One must still wait for all candidates to enter the set, and thus one is constrained by the speed of activation of the slowest entering candidate. This candidate will rarely be the target word and hence will not enter the candidate set any faster than usual. In other words, the verification process should commence at the same time that it would have if the target word had not been repeated. To avoid this problem, one needs to say that candidates enter the verification process as soon as their activation reaches threshold. However, since candidates are verified in order of frequency, this amounts to saying that high frequency words must be activated before low frequency words and therefore the effects of frequency must reside in the activation system.

Once this modification is made to the verification model, we see that it becomes very similar to the search model, except that lexical entries are output to the verification stage on the basis of activation rather than on the basis of a serial matching procedure. Indeed, the two models also have very similar explanations for the next basic effect which we will consider, namely, the semantic priming effect.

THE SEMANTIC PRIMING EFFECT

The search model explains the fact that the response to a word is facilitated when it is preceded by a semantically related word in terms of cross-references that exist in the master file between semantically related words (Forster, 1976, 1979). When a word is accessed, other words which are related to it are made available as a result of a spread of excitation through the semantic network. Forster suggests that at the same time as there is a search for an entry in the peripheral access file, there is a search within the set of semantically delineated words as well. Sometimes the target word is found in this semantic set before it is found in the access file and thus the semantic priming effect occurs.

When access is successful via the semantic set, low frequency words should be treated just like high frequency words since the frequency effect arises from the ordering of entries in the peripheral access file, not the master file. In agreement with this, Becker (1979) observed an attenuation of the frequency effect on words which were preceded by a semantically related word. This result is also in line with the verification account put forward by Becker.

Becker's suggestion is that lexical entries which are semantically related to the prime word are marked off and subjected to the verification process prior to any other lexical entries. The main difference between this and the search model's account is that in Becker's model, the semantic set is checked prior to the sensory defined set rather than in parallel. The implications of this will be discussed in a later chapter, which deals specifically with the influence of semantic context on lexical access.

Semantic priming effects can be explained by the logogen model in terms of semantic features contributing to the activation of logogens. In addition to the sensory features which are extracted from the stimulus word, the logogen system is fed with features extracted from the semantic context. Thus, when the stimulus DOG is presented, it accesses the logogen for DOG which is associated with semantic features like [ANIMAL], [DOMESTIC], [FOUR-LEGGED], etc. These features are then fed into the logogen system so that logogens corresponding to other four-legged domestic animals will experience an increase in activation, even before the next word is read. When CAT is then presented, the sensory features of this word will raise the activation level of the already active logogen for CAT. In this way, fewer sensory features will be required for the threshold level to be reached compared to when CAT has not been preceded by DOG, and thus semantic priming will be observed.

As far as the relationship between semantic priming and frequency goes, the logogen model makes the wrong prediction. The semantic features of a prime word boost the activation level of all related logogens to an extent that depends only on the number of features in common. Therefore, low frequency words which are semantically related to the prime will receive as much of an increase in activation as high frequency words of equivalent relatedness. In other words, the frequency effect should remain the same whether there be semantic priming or not, a prediction not in accord with the findings of Becker (1979).

The interactive-activation model explains semantic priming effects in terms of feedback from semantic level units to word level units (McClelland, 1987). This feedback from the semantic units would increase the activation level of all related word units, including both the prime and the target, and thus there would be lingering activation in the word unit corresponding to the target word when the target word was presented. This is essentially the logogen explanation.

The problem with this account (apart from the wrong prediction about the relationship between frequency and semantic priming) is that inappropriate word units should become de-activated as the appropriate word unit increases in activation. That is, by the time the target word is presented, the unit representing the target word should actually have a low level of activation and produce inhibition rather than facilitation (as has been previously suggested as an explanation for the possible inhibitory effects of form-related pairs like LOOK and BOOK). In other words, when DOG is presented, the unit for DOG will become activated which, in turn, will activate the DOMESTIC ANIMAL semantic unit. This will then feed back to all the word units that are positively linked to the DOMESTIC ANIMAL unit (i.e. DOG, CAT, etc.) which will consequently be increased in activation. However, since the word units DOG and CAT will be competing at the same level, and since the sensory information supports the activation of DOG, the word unit for CAT will become de-activated. Therefore, when the word CAT is presented there should be no facilitation, and in fact, there could be inhibition. Given that facilitation is invariably observed, it seems that the locus of semantic priming effects in the interactive-activation model needs further consideration.

THE DEGRADATION EFFECT

The delay in response times caused by degradation of the stimulus item could be accommodated by the search model at the initial encoding stage when a sensory representation is being established for use in the lexical search. That is, a transformation of the stimulus into some sort of uniform, clear format would be required for a sensory-to-lexical match to be achieved. In addition, there could be an effect of degradation on the stage when the accessed lexical entry is checked back to the original stimulus.

An attempt has been made to determine the locus of the degradation effect by examining its interaction with the frequency effect and the lexical status effect. If degradation influences an initial normalization stage, then all stimuli should be equally affected by it. That is, high frequency words, low frequency words, and nonwords should all produce a degradation effect of equal magnitude. Such a constant effect of degradation on words of different frequency was observed by Stanners et al. (1975) using a dot pattern mask, Becker and Killion (1977) using variations in stimulus intensity, and by Besner (1983) and Besner and McCann (1987) using case alternation. However, Besner also found that lexical decision times to nonwords were less affected by case alternation than those to words. This interaction between degradation and lexical status can be explained, however, if one assumes that degradation also affects the post-access checking stage. Nonwords do not enter the checking stage unless they are sufficiently wordlike to access a lexical entry. Therefore, words would be affected by case alternation at two loci, while unwordlike nonwords would be affected at only one. Kinoshita (1987) employed nonwords which were much more wordlike than those used by Besner, and did obtain a much larger effect of case alternation on the nonwords, as would be expected by this account.

The verification model provides a similar explanation for degradation effects as the search model, since the effects could arise at both the pre-access letter processing stage and the verification stage. However, there are differences in the predictions of the two models arising from the difference in the nature of the verification stage. In the search model, the first candidate that is checked will usually be the correct word regardless of its frequency. Other candidates only enter the checking stage when the stimulus is very similar to more than one word. In the verification model, on the other hand, the verification set will typically contain a number of candidates which will be verified in order of frequency.

If degradation of the stimulus means that each attempt at verification will take longer than normal, then the verification model predicts a greater effect of degradation on low frequency words than high frequency words since more candidates must be checked, and this prediction is not upheld. The effect of degradation on legal nonwords would depend on how many words there were in the candidate set. If there were many (i.e. if the nonword were very wordlike), the effect of degradation could be even larger for nonwords than for words, which is the trend that Kinoshita observed. To explain all of the data though, in particular the additivity of frequency and degradation, the verification model needs to reconsider the nature of the candidate set.

There are two ways in which the logogen model (and interactive-activation model) would be able to explain the degradation effect. The most commonly cited explanation (e.g. Henderson, 1982; Mitchell, 1982) is that the extraction of sensory evidence to be fed into the logogens is slower when the stimulus is degraded. According to this account, there will be an increasingly larger effect of degradation the more the sensory evidence that is required before a response can be made. In other words, low frequency words should show a greater effect of degradation than high frequency words, and nonwords should show an even greater effect. As we have just seen, however, the effects of frequency and degradation do not interact and the relationship between lexical status and degradation is variable, perhaps depending on the similarity of the nonword to a word.

The logogen model does have a second way of explaining degradation effects (as pointed out by Besner & McCann, 1987), which at least correctly predicts the additive effects of frequency and degradation. As was previously suggested in relation to the search and verification models, the stimulus could be normalized in some way prior to the stimulus characteristics being fed into the lexical system. The same normalization occurs regardless of the frequency or the lexical status of the stimulus item. Where the logogen model runs into problems, however, is in the variable effects observed with nonwords.

The search and verification models were able to incorporate these effects at the post-access verification stage of lexical processing. If we accept the claim made earlier that the logogen and interactive-activation models need to include a post-access checking stage in order to account for word similarity effects on nonword responses, then these models are able to explain the degradation effects in the same way as the search model does. That is, there are two loci for the effect; an initial normalization stage and a post-access checking stage.

OVERVIEW OF THE STRENGTHS AND
WEAKNESSES OF THE MODELS

It is seen in the above discussion that the search model is able to explain at least the basic phenomena observed using the lexical decision task. Where the model encounters major problems is in explaining the facilitative effects of large neighbourhood size, and also some of the effects of form priming which Forster himself has uncovered, particularly the occasional inhibitory effects produced by a form-related prime. In addition, if it were convincingly shown that the response to a high frequency word is affected by the similarity of that word to a lower frequency word (e.g. MINUTE being similar to MINUET), then the search model would need reconsideration. It would be necessary to say that the search continues on after an entry has been accessed (see Forster, 1989, for a discussion of the implications of such a modification).

Aside from the these potential empirical problems, the search model seems to have become unfashionable in recent times for theoretical reasons. Lexical access would be a slow and cumbersome process if the entire lexicon were searched for every word encountered in a sentence, and therefore some way of reducing the size of the search set is required. The notion of "bins", which Forster puts forward to accommodate this requirement, has not been given much theoretical consideration, even by Forster, and has received little or no empirical support. If words are grouped together in bins on the basis of their first and last letter (as Forster suggests) then disruption of the first or last letter should lead to a failure to access the word. However, Chambers (1979) has demonstrated delayed reaction times to words which are created by transposing the first two letters of another word. For example, the word

LATITUDE which is generated from ALTITUDE takes longer to recognize than the control word PETITION, suggesting that the lexical entry for ALTITUDE is inappropriately accessed when LATITUDE is presented. A bin system which incorporates the first letter in its organizational code, would not have the word ALTITUDE in the same bin that is examined when LATITUDE is presented, and therefore no interference should ensue. If the notion of bins is to become more widely accepted, therefore, the details of their organization and structure will need to be elaborated and substantiated.

Given the lack of appeal of the bin notion, a different means of reducing the set of potential candidates has been sought, and the favoured position has been the involvement of logogen-type activation process. One advantage of activation as the method for narrowing down the number of lexical entries that are worth considering, is that it provides an account of approximate sensory-to-lexical matching.

The search model is rather vague about how approximate matches are made. If a lexical entry is found to be sufficiently similar to the incoming sensory information, then it is accessed and enters the post-access checking stage. This similarity decision must presumably be based on the number of orthographic features which the stimulus and the lexical representation have in common. If the number of features in common reaches some criterion value, then the lexical entry will be accessed.

The requirement that there be a criterion for accepting a sensory-to-lexical match, is essentially equivalent to an activation view. That is, features of the sensory input activate a lexical entry to a certain level and if this level exceeds a criterion value, the entry can enter the verification stage. Therefore, an activation mechanism is able to explain neatly how approximate matches are made, while providing an account of lexical access that does not require that a huge number of irrelevant entries be given consideration.

The above discussion, therefore, comes out in favour of an activation model, though one which has an additional post-access checking stage. This additional stage is required to explain why word similarity effects are sometimes reflected in response times, but not in errors (i.e. in the case of letter substituted nonwords like KONDERGARTEN or MUSIT), and also to explain how the effect of degradation on nonword items can be weaker than the effect on word items (and how the former varies depending upon the wordlikeness of the nonword).

One such activation-plus-checking model is the verification model, but it is also possible to add a checking stage to the logogen and interactive-activation models, as outlined earlier. It may be that a lexical entry is activated via a logogen or interactive-activation system and then that entry is checked back to the original stimulus. The difference between the verification model and the logogen and interactive-activation models is that the checking stage of the former is essential for choosing amongst an activated set of candidates, while the checking stage proposed for the latter is merely used to confirm whether a single activated entry is appropriate or not. Hence, the checking stage is an integral part of the verification model, whereas it is an optional mechanism for the other activation models and is only really necessary when there is some likelihood that an accessed entry could be inappropriate.

Even with the additional assumption of a checking stage, the activation models have difficulties explaining the pattern of masked form-priming observed by Forster (1987), although this is a problem for any of the current models of lexical access. Further, though, the logogen model incorrectly predicts an additive effect of frequency and semantic relatedness, while the interactive-activation model cannot explain the semantic relatedness effect at all, given the nature of its inhibitory mechanism. Clearly, these activation models must reconsider the way they account for the influence of semantics on lexical access. The influence of semantic context on lexical processing will be discussed in depth in the next chapter where it will be shown that semantic context effects appear to arise primarily at a post-access stage of processing. The activation models could incorporate this notion without abandoning their essential character; they need only abandon their account of where semantic feedback fits into the system.

Since the verification model provides the best explanation of semantic priming effects as they have been described so far, it may seem that such a model should be favoured over the other activation models. However, in the next chapter, we will see that, on closer scrutiny, the verification model is found wanting. In addition, the verification model faces the same problems as does the search model in explaining the neighbourhood size effect and the possible delay in responses to a high frequency word arising from its similarity to a low frequency word.

IS THE LEXICAL DECISION TASK APPROPRIATE?

Before moving on to the issue of semantic effects on lexical processing, a final point must be considered in relation to the interpretation of experiments which purport to evaluate models of lexical access. Specifically, many of the experiments make use of the lexical decision task for reasons outlined in the previous chapter. However, not everyone accepts that this task is a suitable way of tapping into lexical access mechanisms.

Balota and Chumbley (1984, 1985) were the first to bring this issue to prominence, by claiming that at least one of the basic effects, namely, the frequency effect, could arise at the post-access decision stage rather than during the course of lexical access *per se*. If true, this would mean that the lexical decision task might be gauging task-specific effects that have little to do with normal lexical access during reading. The evidence that Balota and Chumbley provide for their claim that the lexical decision task is an inappropriate way of measuring lexical access, is that the frequency effect appears to be absent in other tasks.

They argue that if the frequency effect emanates from the process of gaining access to a lexical entry, then any responses that are made on the basis of accessing information contained within that lexical entry must be sensitive to word frequency. Examples of information contained within a lexical entry are the meaning and the pronunciation of the word. Therefore, the time taken to decide that a word belongs to a particular semantic category and the time taken to initiate the pronunciation of a word should both be correlated with word frequency. Contrary to this, however, Balota and Chumbley (1984) observed no significant relationship between frequency and semantic categorization times and only a weak relationship between frequency and naming times. The weak effect of frequency on naming responses was later ascribed to that stage of processing where the articulatory representation is set up for verbal output (Balota & Chumbley, 1985), since a frequency effect was observed on naming times even when the subjects had plenty of time to identify the word prior to the naming response being elicited (i.e. on delayed naming times).

As a result of their findings from the semantic categorization and naming tasks, Balota and Chumbley concluded that the frequency effect observed in the lexical decision task must arise at a post-access decision stage specific to that task. Such a stage could be seen as being equivalent to the optional checking stage which was postulated as being a necessary adjunct to the activation models. However, one's conception of the initial activation stage would be fundamentally affected if it were concluded that the frequency effect arose at this checking stage rather than at the activation stage.

As it happens though, strong arguments have been mounted against Balota and Chumbley's conclusions (e.g. Monsell, Doyle, & Haggard, 1989; Paap et al., 1987). Turning first to the semantic categorization task, one possible explanation for Balota and Chumbley's failure to find a significant frequency effect could be given along the same lines as Becker's explanation for the attenuation of frequency in the semantic priming task. When the category is presented (e.g. FRUIT), it may be the case that a set of exemplars of that category is extracted from semantic memory and this semantically defined set is initially accessed when the target word (e.g. APPLE) is presented. If the word is found within this set, a positive response can be made, and since the semantically defined set is more likely to be sensitive to category typicality than word frequency, there is no reason to expect the response to show a frequency effect. Consistent with this is the fact that Monsell et al. found a strong frequency effect on a semantic categorization task when the semantic categories were very large (namely, animate versus inanimate), where there is no advantage in setting up a semantically defined set.

As far as the naming response goes, the frequency effect could be reduced compared to lexical decision simply because it is often possible to get the naming response underway on the basis of non-lexical information. For example, the initial part of the word APPLE could be prepared for articulation on the basis of the way that APP would be pronounced by letter-to-sound rules (which will be discussed in greater detail in Chapter 4). Only for words with unpredictable initial pronunciations would such a strategy be unsuccessful (e.g. irregular words like CHASM or THYME, or words with unstressed first syllables, like CIGAR). Monsell et al. provide support for such an idea in that they observed just as strong an effect of frequency in naming as in lexical decision for words with an unstressed first syllable (like CIGAR), while words with a predictable initial segment, that is, with stress on their first syllable (e.g. HERON), showed a stronger effect of frequency in lexical decision than in naming.

Finally, the finding of a frequency effect in the delayed naming task could be explained because subjects were re-processing the words prior to naming them. Under conditions where such re-processing would be minimized, Monsell et al. (1989) were able to eliminate the frequency effect in the delayed naming task (see also Savage, Bradley, & Forster, 1990, who failed to find frequency effects, but did find lexicality effects, in the delayed naming task).

McCann and Besner (1987) and McCann, Besner, and Davelaar (1988) have also argued that frequency effects do not arise during access, but rather, arise from the familiarity of the stimulus or from the familiarity of its phonological form, as determined post-lexically. Their argument was largely based on the fact that the latency to name a "pseudohomophone" (i.e. a nonword, like BRANE, which is pronounced identically to a word) was unaffected by the frequency of the word to which it was homophonic (McCann and Besner, 1987). On the other hand, frequency did affect the time taken to say that the psuedohomophone was pronounced identically to a word (McCann et al., 1988). The claim was made from these findings that frequency effects arise during a familiar/unfamiliar discrimination process, which is a post-access stage that is required in making a lexical decision and a homophone decision, but not in making a naming response. One cannot explain the failure to find a frequency effect in the naming task in terms of the application of spelling-to-sound rules washing out the effect, since the task revealed that pseudohomophones were named faster than non-homophones, suggesting that lexical information did affect response times.

It was the case, however, that the orthographic similarity of the pseudohomophones to real words was not controlled and, since this is an important influence on the determination of the pronunciation of a pseudohomophone (McCann et al., 1988; Taft, 1982), it is very possible that this factor washed out the frequency effect.

In a recent unpublished study in the author's own laboratory, both naming latencies and homophone decision latencies for pseudo-homophones were collected, and while the experiment was not specifically set up to examine frequency effects, the correlation between latencies and frequency was much the same in the two tasks (0.25 for naming and 0.28 for homophone decision). The fact that in neither case was the correlation very strong presumably reflects the contamination of the orthographic similarity factor. Of course, it would be very easy to test McCann and Besner's claim directly by matching "high frequency" and "low frequency" pseudohomophones on orthographic similarity (e.g. BRANE versus SLANE) and seeing whether the frequency effect is eliminated in the naming task.

There is, in fact, evidence from a completely different experimental paradigm that supports the view that word frequency effects do not arise from any task-specific decision processes. If one measures the length of time that a reader spends looking at a particular word while reading a passage of text, one finds that less time is spent on high than on low frequency words (e.g. Inhoff & Rayner, 1986; Just & Carpenter, 1980; Rayner & Duffy, 1986) although the effect is not necessarily strong (Underwood, Hubbard, & Wilkinson, 1990). Such a result affirms the importance of word frequency in the lexical access process, since no decision is required in the task; the subject simply reads the text in the normal manner.

All in all then, there is little support for the claim that the lexical decision task is a poor measure of lexical access. It is important to acknowledge, however, that the lexical decision task does include a post-access decision stage and consideration must always be given to the possibility that any effect obtained in that task could have arisen at this task-specific stage of processing. It will be seen in what follows that naming times are often compared to lexical decision times in order to gauge the importance of post-access factors.

NOTE

1. It should be pointed out that Morton only intended the logogen model to be applied to tachistoscopic recognition and not to lexical decision. This latter application has been adopted by others (e.g. M.Coltheart et al., 1977)

CHAPTER THREE

Semantic and Syntactic Influences in Lexical Processing

Within the interactive-activation framework, it is possible for the semantic and syntactic characteristics of a word (i.e. its meaning, its part of speech, etc.) to play a role during lexical access, since there is feedback from higher levels down to lower levels during the access process. According to the other models, semantic and syntactic information about a word is made available only once its lexical entry has been accessed, and therefore, this information would not be expected to affect the lexical retrieval process itself.

The evidence is that the semantic and syntactic characteristics of a word do influence lexical decision responses. However, it is likely that this influence arises at the post-access decision stage of the response (i.e. the stage where one answers the question: "Does the locating of a lexical entry mean that the presented item is actually a word?"). This will now be examined.

SEMANTIC CHARACTERISTICS OF ISOLATED WORDS

Concreteness

Whaley (1978), in a regression analysis of lexical decision times, found that a substantial amount of variance was explained by a "richness of meaning" factor which included concreteness and meaningfulness. The "meaningfulness" of a word was a measure of the number of words that could be thought of as associates of that word within a set amount of time. "Concreteness" was based on ratings reported by Paivio, Yuille, and Madigan (1968). In a direct comparison of concrete and abstract words (e.g. BONE versus FATE), James (1975) observed a speed advantage in lexical decision responses for concrete words, although only when of low frequency.

Questioning whether such a concreteness effect means that concrete and abstract words are accessed differently in the lexicon, Kroll and Merves (1986) were able to manipulate the concreteness effect by manipulating the presentation conditions. The fact that the concreteness effect seemed to be under strategic control was taken as support for the idea that the difference between abstract and concrete words arises, not from differential lexical organization, but from information gathered from the lexical entry after it has been accessed. This information influences the post-access decision stage of the lexical decision response.

In support of this sort of post-access interpretation, Schwanenflugel and Shoben (1983) eliminated the concreteness effect when the words were placed in a sentential context. They suggested that it is more difficult to decide that an isolated abstract word is a word than to decide that an isolated concrete word is a word, because the meaning of an abstract word is heavily dependent upon the context in which it normally appears. The meaning of a concrete word is typically less context-dependent. By placing an abstract word into a sentence, one provides the context in which the word is so heavily dependent, thus eliminating the concreteness effect.

It should be noted, however, that an effect of concreteness has been obtained using a naming task as well as a lexical decision task (Bleasdale, 1987) and therefore it may actually be the case that the concreteness effect does arise from a difference in lexical organization between abstract and concrete words, rather than at the decision phase. The account proffered by Bleasdale (1983, 1987) emanates from the dual-coding theory of Paivio (1971) whereby concrete words are represented in both a verbally-based lexicon and an image-based lexicon. Since abstract words are represented in the verbally-based lexicon only, there is a greater chance of locating a concrete word than an abstract word if both lexicons are consulted.

Polysemy

Jastrzembski (1981) has argued that the concreteness variable has been confounded with another semantic variable. He suggests that concrete words have more meanings than abstract words and that it is this factor that leads to the supposed concreteness effect. The more meanings a word has, the faster the recognition times are found to be (as also demonstrated by H. Rubenstein et al., 1970, 1971b; and Jastrzembski & Stanners, 1975). These investigators propose that each meaning of a word has its own lexical entry and, the more entries that could potentially match with the presented letter string, the greater the probability of accessing an appropriate entry within a particular period of time. Thus, response times will be faster for polysemous words (i.e. words with more than one meaning) compared to non-ambiguous words. However, if this polysemy effect arises from lexical organization rather than from post-access decision processes, the effect should also be observed for naming responses. On the contrary, Chumbley and Balota (1984) found no effect of polysemy on naming times, despite finding an effect on lexical decision times. Therefore, polysemy seems to play its role when deciding whether a letter string is actually a word or not.

On the other hand, Gernsbacher (1984) has claimed that both the facilitatory effect of polysemy and of concreteness can be accounted for by yet another confounding variable. This variable is "word familiarity", as based on subjective ratings.

Subjective Familiarity

Gernsbacher (1984) demonstrated that when rated familiarity is controlled in a lexical decision task, both the effect of polysemy and the effect of concreteness disappear. That is, polysemous and concrete words tend to be more familiar than the word frequency norms would suggest, so that it would seem to be more appropriate to match items on subjective familiarity rather than on the objective word frequency provided by word frequency norms like Kučera and Francis (1967) and Carroll, Davies, and Richman (1971).

Although it is conceivable that Gernsbacher's observations do account for all of the putative semantic effects in isolated word recognition, there needs to be considerable caution exercised in interpreting experiments which match items on rated subjective familiarity ratings rather than on objective frequency. The problem is that it is possible that raters base their feeling of familiarity on a sense of how long it takes to recognize a word. If, for example, a rater is able to access a concrete word more quickly than an abstract word matched on objective frequency, the former might be rated as being more familiar than the latter. Therefore, in order to match a concrete word with an abstract word on familiarity, one must use a concrete word which is of lower frequency than the matched abstract word and this could wash out any genuine effect of concreteness. In other words, matching two words on their subjective familiarity might be tantamount to matching those words on their access times and, hence, it is hardly surprising that the words fail to differ in their response times.

In summary, it is unclear whether word recognition is influenced by the semantic characteristics of the word or not, but if it is, there are two possible sources of influence. Either it is the decision that the letter string is a word that is affected (e.g. Chumbley & Balota, 1984; Kroll & Merves, 1986; Schwanenflugel & Shoben, 1983; Taft, 1990), or it is the case that words with different semantic characteristics are represented differentially in the lexicon (e.g. Bleasdale, 1983, 1987; Jastrzembski, 1981). Turning now to syntactic influences in the recognition of isolated words, the same two sources of influence are also possible.

WORD CLASS

There appear to be no studies which report any reliable difference in access times between nouns, verbs, and adjectives. Where syntactic effects have been reported has been in the contrast between "open class" words (i.e. nouns, verbs, and adjectives) and "closed class" words (i.e. the minor lexical classes, such as articles, prepositions, quantifiers, conjunctions, and auxiliaries).

Bradley (1978) reported two paradigms in which open and closed class words appeared to differ in their lexical decision times. In the first of these, closed class words were found to be insensitive to word frequency, unlike open class words. However, many subsequent experiments have failed to support this finding (e.g. Gordon & Carramazza, 1982, 1983, 1985; Matthei & Kean, 1989; Segui, Mehler, Frauenfelder, & Morton, 1982; Taft, 1990). The second paradigm appears to be more robust. It was found that the interference effect which arises from the presence of a word at the beginning of a nonword (Taft & Forster, 1976) was only present when that word belonged to the open class, and not to the closed class. For example, while there was a delay in lexical decision responses to SETITUDE compared to DITITUDE (with SET being an open class word), there was no delay in responses to YETITUDE, where YET is a closed class word. This result has been replicated by Kolk and Blomert (1985), Shapiro and Jensen (1986), and Matthei and Kean (1989), although not by Petocz and Oliphant (1988).

Bradley's explanation for this apparent differential processing of open and closed class words is that the standard lexicon is supplemented by a specialized closed class lexicon, which has properties that are different to the standard lexicon. Bringing this closed class lexicon into play during access must be under strategic control, since Kolk and

Blomert (1985) were able to make the nonword interference effect come and go for closed class items depending upon the experimental conditions. However, rather than offering an organizational account of the differences between open and closed class words, it is possible that the differences arise from the post-access decision phase (e.g. Matthei & Kean, 1989), just as was suggested for semantic effects on word recognition.

Consistent with this view is the fact that Taft (1990) found that lexical decision times for function words (i.e. closed class words whose definition can only be given in terms of their syntactic function, like THAN and NOR) were longer than those for open class words, but that naming times revealed no such difference. On the other hand, differential processing of open class and closed class words has also been observed in a letter cancellation task (Rosenberg, Zurif, Brownell, Garrett, & Bradley, 1985) and a word monitoring task (Swinney, Zurif, & Cutler, 1980; Friederici, 1985), neither of which would seem to warrant the same sort of post-access decision processes inherent in the lexical decision task. Since Taft's result can actually be interpreted as being a semantic effect rather than a syntactic one (see Taft, 1990), Bradley's syntactically based dual-lexicon account is not necessarily undermined by the different pattern of results obtained in the lexical decision and naming tasks. However, given the failure to replicate her frequency sensitivity result, both lexicons must be said to at least share the property of being sensitive to word frequency.

BEYOND THE ISOLATED WORD

The focus until this point has been on the issue of how a reader decodes an isolated, visually presented letter string. However, the most common situation in which the reader is confronted with a word to decode, is where that word must be comprehended within the context of other words. Semantic and syntactic factors would seem to be most relevent in word recognition when the word is considered within its normal sentence environment. It is possible, in fact, that the processes involved in accessing a word in the lexicon are qualitatively quite different when that word is presented in a sentence context compared to when it is presented in isolation. If this turns out to be so, what I have talked about up until now will be of little interest to anyone concerned with the decoding of words in normal reading. If, on the other hand, it can be shown that lexical access of a word in context is equivalent to lexical access of that word in isolation, then what I have covered so far does have a lot to say about the normal reading process. Fortunately, it is the latter position that the evidence points to. First, let us look at the influence of the semantic context in word recognition.

TACHISTOSCOPIC RECOGNITION OF WORDS IN CONTEXT

Perhaps the first demonstration that semantic context influences the identification of a visually presented word was reported by O'Neil in 1953. He demonstrated that tachistoscopic identification was facilitated by the prior exposure of a semantically associated word (e.g. identification of NURSE being facilitated by the prior presentation of DOCTOR).

The same sort of result was subsequently obtained using a sentence fragment as the context that was exposed prior to the tachistoscopically presented target word (e.g. Morton, 1964; Tulving & Gold, 1963). For example, one requires less exposure time to identify the word MIRROR when one has been presented with the sentence fragment HE SPENT HOURS LOOKING AT HIMSELF IN THE, than when one is not presented with any prior context.

To conclude from these studies that word recognition is fundamentally altered by the presence of context is, however, misleading. As pointed out in Chapter 1, the tachistoscopic identification task may well be measuring something other than on-line lexical processing. In particular, by presenting a degraded stimulus, one is forcing subjects to guess what the word might be and obviously such a guessing strategy will be facilitated by the presence of relevant contextual cues. In fact, if the context is sufficiently predictive, the target word need not even be presented at all for the subject to give the right answer, and this could hardly be called word recognition.

SINGLE WORD CONTEXTS

Semantic Priming

The concept of semantic priming was introduced in Chapter 1. Meyer and Schvaneveldt (1971) were the first to demonstrate in an on-line task (the lexical decision task), that responses to a target word (e.g. NURSE) were facilitated when preceded by a semantically related prime (e.g. DOCTOR) compared to when preceded by an unrelated word (e.g. NATION). The explanation given by Meyer and Schvaneveldt for this semantic priming effect was that activation automatically spreads from an accessed lexical entry to other lexical entries that are semantically related to it. This spread of activation results in a relatively fast access time for any of the activated words should they now be presented for recognition. While others have supported the existence of an automatic spreading activation mechanism (e.g. Fischler, 1977; Fischler & Goodman, 1978; Neely, 1976),[1] there is evidence to suggest that additional mechanisms are at play (e.g. Antos, 1979; de Groot, 1983, 1984; Neely, 1976, 1977; Seidenberg, Waters, Sanders, & Langer, 1984a; Tweedy, Lapinski, & Schvaneveldt, 1977; Tweedy & Lapinski, 1981).

The Two-process Model

The most influential suggestion for an additional mechanism comes from Neely (1976, 1977). Neely (1976) examined lexical decision times to targets which were either preceded by a related word (e.g. DOCTOR NURSE), an unrelated word (e.g. NATION NURSE) or a neutral stimulus, namely, a row of X's (e.g. XXXXXX NURSE). What Neely found was that, while the targets in the "related" condition were faster than the targets in the "neutral" condition, the targets in the "unrelated" condition were actually slower than those in the neutral condition. In other words, responses were inhibited when the prime and target were semantically unrelated. There is no reason for an automatic spreading activation process to produce inhibition when the prime and the target are unrelated as the target word will simply remain unactivated, just as it would in the neutral condition. In order to explain the inhibitory effect for unrelated words, as well as the facilitatory effect for related words, Neely expanded upon the two-process model of expectancy put forward by Posner and Snyder (1975).

In addition to the spreading activation process, subjects have available to them a conscious attentional strategy. This conscious strategy develops slowly and involves directing one's attention to that area of lexical memory which is associated with the domain of semantic memory that relates to the meaning of the previously accessed word. If the target word is not to be found in this area of lexical memory, subjects will be biased toward thinking that the target is not a word and therefore the correct lexical decision response to the target word will be delayed. On the other hand, lexical decision responses will be facilitated if the target word is located in the circumscribed area of lexical memory.

Since the attentional strategy takes time to develop, it follows that its influence will only be observed (in the form of an inhibitory effect for unrelated words) if there is time enough for it to develop before the response is made. In support of this, Neely (1977) demonstrated an inhibitory effect only when the delay between the prime and the target was relatively long. Further support for the idea that the inhibitory effect arises from an attentional strategy comes from the finding by

Forster (1981) and Lorch, Balota, and Stamm (1986) that facilitation, but not inhibition, is observed when naming times are measured. In the naming task there is no word/nonword decision required and therefore little opportunity for the attentional decision bias to play a role. Facilitation of response times to words preceded by a semantically related prime therefore appears to result from an automatic spread of activation to the lexical entry for the target word.

The Verification Model

There is an alternative account for the pattern of facilitation and inhibition observed in semantic priming studies. This is the explanation given by the verification model of lexical access (e.g. Becker, 1976; Becker & Killion, 1977). According to this model, a set of candidate lexical entries is activated and this set is then searched through to find an entry which matches the presented stimulus. As outlined in Chapter 2, semantic priming results are explained in the following way (e.g. Becker, 1979, 1980, 1985).

After a word has been accessed, other associated words are accessed as well, either through spreading activation (e.g. Becker, 1979) or through a cross-referencing system (Forster, 1976). These other words form a "semantically determined" set which can be searched through when a new word is presented. If the new word is found within this semantically determined set, then normal access within the lexicon itself (i.e. a search through a "sensorily determined" set) is short-circuited. Since the semantically determined set is likely to be smaller than the sensorily determined set, response times are faster if the word is found within the former. A target in a neutral context (e.g. following a row of X's) will be found within the sensorily determined set, since no semantically determined set will have been set up. However, a target which is semantically related to a prime word will be found within the smaller semantically determined set, and therefore facilitation will be observed relative to the neutral condition. Inhibition arises from the fact that a semantic set is generated from the context, but that the unrelated target is not found in this set and is only found subsequently in the sensory set. Therefore, response times will be delayed relative to a neutral condition where no inappropriate semantic set has been generated.

Several predictions emerge from the verification model. First, since the semantically determined set will be organized semantically rather than on the basis of word frequency, there is no reason to expect the frequency of the word to influence response times when it is found in the semantic set. This prediction was partly supported by Becker (1979) who found a reduction in the size of the frequency effect for words in context. Although the frequency effect was significant even when the word was in context, this can be explained by saying that the related targets were not always to be found in the semantic set for all of the subjects.

The second prediction arising from the verification model is that the larger the semantic set, the smaller the advantage of finding the word in this set rather than in the sensory set, and therefore the smaller the facilitation effect. Furthermore, since the inhibition effect reflects the time taken to inspect the semantic set, the larger this set, the greater should be the inhibition. Becker (1980) confirmed this prediction of weaker facilitation and greater inhibition when the context defined a large set as opposed to a small set. To generate a large set, the single word context formed a category name, as in BIRD ROBIN (related) or FLOWER WRIST (unrelated), whereas the small set was generated by using antonyms (e.g. HOT COLD).

There is one prediction that the verification model makes, however, that is not supported by the available data. If the target that follows the word prime is a nonword, there should be an attempt to locate the nonword in the semantically defined set prior to determining that it does not also exist in the sensorily defined set. There is no way of knowing whether the letter string that is being searched for in the semantic set is actually a word or not. Because of this, it should be the case that a nonword is responded to more slowly in a lexical decision task when it is preceded by a word than when it is preceded by a row of X's. In the event, however, the opposite is the case (Neely, 1976), a finding which makes little sense in terms of the verification model. On the other hand, the observed nonword facilitation effect can be explained in terms of the two-process model. A nonword target will not be found in that part of lexical memory which is circumscribed by the context and, therefore, there will be a bias toward thinking that the target is not a word, and this will lead to a faster nonword response compared to when there is no context.

It is apparent from the above discussion that access to a word is fundamentally altered when that word is preceded by a semantically related word. However, while this might be the case when the two words are presented in isolation, we can ask if it is also true in the more naturalistic setting where the associatively related words are contained in a sentence. That is, is NURSE more readily responded to when it occurs in the sentence THE DOCTOR LIKED THE NURSE than when it occurs in the sentence THE LAWYER LIKED THE NURSE, since DOCTOR and NURSE are associatively related while LAWYER and NURSE are not? Forster (1979) cites a study by Bodi (1977) which answers this question negatively, suggesting that the associative relatedness effect is lost when the related words are placed in a sentence framework. Simpson, Peterson, Casteel, and Burgess (1989) similarly found no effect of semantic association using sentence contexts.

This does not mean, however, that the recognition of a word is therefore not affected by the sentence context. For example, it may be the case that NURSE is more rapidly responded to when it is preceded by a sensible sentence context like THE LAWYER LIKED THE than by an anomalous sentence context like THE CARROT SMOKED THE. What follows is a discussion of whether this is the case and, if so, how it should be interpreted.

SENTENCE CONTEXTS

A Possible Mechanism for Sentence Context Effects

While it is easy to envisage a lexical memory system set up in such a way that associated words are linked together, it is less obvious how lexical memory would be set up to allow sentence fragments to be linked to associated words. In other words, it may be the case that responses to NURSE are facilitated when preceded by DOCTOR because activation can spread between their lexical entries; but as there is no lexical entry for WHEN SHE GREW UP SHE WANTED TO BECOME A, there is no reason for responses to NURSE to be facilitated when placed in this context. Furthermore, there are no individual words in the sentence fragment WHEN SHE GREW UP SHE WANTED TO BECOME A which are likely to have lexical entries that are linked to the lexical entry for the word NURSE (except, perhaps, SHE).

This sort of logical argument was strongly made by Forster (1976, 1981) to counter the idea that a sentence context can predispose the lexical access system to anticipate a particular word. However, there is an alternative to the notion that such a predisposition only arises from the spread of activation from one lexical entry to another. It is possible that activation of a lexical entry can spread from some sort of propositional sub-structure in semantic memory (e.g. Foss, 1982), whereby a schema for "female professions" is activated by the presentation of WHEN SHE GREW UP SHE WANTED TO BECOME A and this schema is linked to the lexical entry for NURSE, which then becomes activated. It is therefore conceivable that lexical access is indeed altered by the presence of a sentential context; but does the empirical research support such a notion?

Experimental Studies of Sentence Context Effects

It was Schuberth and Eimas (1977) who first published an effect of sentence context on the on-line processing of visually presented words. Subjects were presented with a target word (e.g. BONE) following a brief presentation of a sentence fragment which was either congruent with the target word (e.g. THE DOG GNAWED HAPPILY ON THE) or incongruent with it (e.g. THE GIRL RAN HURRIEDLY THROUGH THE). Subjects were required to make a lexical decision response by deciding whether the target item was a word or not. Comparing lexical decision times under these conditions to a neutral condition where the word was not preceded by any sentence fragment at all, Schuberth and Eimas found that the congruous contexts led to faster responses and the incongruous contexts led to slower responses. In other words, they replicated Neely's finding of facilitation for congruent targets and inhibition for incongruent targets using sentence fragments as the context rather than single words. The results of Schuberth and Eimas are therefore in accord with the two-process model advocated by Neely to explain his results: Both automatic spreading activation and a conscious attentional strategy lead to facilitation when the target is congruous with the context, but the conscious attentional strategy also leads to inhibition when the target is incongruous with the context.

Now, since the facilitation effect arises at least partly from the spread of activation, one might expect to observe a facilitation effect even when the target is not the most predictable word given the context. In fact, Fischler (1977), Koriat (1981), and Forster (1981) upheld this expectation using single word contexts (e.g. NURSE is facilitated by the prior presentation of INJECTION as well as DOCTOR). However, Schuberth and Eimas only used highly predictable congruent targets, so we do not know from their study if the facilitation effect would be maintained in a situation where the word is acceptable in the sentential context, but is not highly predictable, e.g. the word BONE following the sentence fragment INSIDE THE CAVE THEY FOUND A LARGE. In fact, these sort of sentences are far more common in the normal reading setting than are sentences where a word is highly predictable from the semantic context.

Fischler and Bloom (1979) ran a series of experiments using sentence contexts from which they were able to conclude that congruous targets produce facilitation relative to a neutral condition only when the target is highly predictable from the context. In other words, recognition of BONE is facilitated by the prior presentation of THE DOG GNAWED HAPPILY ON THE, but is not facilitated by the prior presentation of INSIDE THE CAVE THEY FOUND A LARGE. Since Fischler and

Bloom also obtained inhibition effects when the target was incongruent with the context, the two-process view would have to hold that only the conscious attentional strategy is employed in a sentential context. This strategy will produce inhibition, but will only produce facilitation when attention is successfully directed to the target word on the basis of the context, namely, when the target is highly predictable from the context. However, as Fischler and Bloom point out, it should actually be the case that if a word is not predictable in the context, regardless of whether it is acceptable in the context or not, there should be a bias toward saying that it is not a word and therefore inhibition should be observed. Therefore, the acceptable although unpredictable targets should have been responded to more slowly than the neutral targets, but they were not. In other words, it is difficult for the two-process model to account for results which fail to demonstrate a facilitation effect for congruous targets while at the same time demonstrating an inhibition effect for incongruous targets.

From an extensive series of experiments, however, Stanovich and West have come out in favour of the two-process model (Stanovich, 1980, 1981; Stanovich & West, 1979, 1981, 1983; West & Stanovich, 1978, 1982). The data that they produce appear to be at odds with those of Fischler and Bloom (1979). Using highly predictable congruous targets, West and Stanovich (1978) and Stanovich and West (1979) observed a facilitation effect but no inhibition effect under normal presentation conditions. A significant inhibition effect only emerged when the target word was delayed or degraded or when the subjects were poor readers. Furthermore, Stanovich and West (1981) obtained a facilitation effect even when the congruous targets were not highly predictable from the context.

These data are exactly what the two-process model predicts. Facilitation arises from spreading activation, so that words will be primed by most contexts in which they are acceptable. Inhibition arises from the attentional strategy which is slow-acting and hence only comes into play when there is a sufficient delay in gaining access to the word via its sensory representation (e.g. when the target is degraded or when the reader has poor decoding skills).

How do we resolve the conflict between the results of Stanovich and West and those of Fischler and Bloom? In particular, under normal presentation conditions using normal adult readers, Stanovich and West found facilitation for all acceptable contexts, but no inhibition for unacceptable contexts, whereas Fischler and Bloom found facilitation for predictable contexts only, as well as inhibition for unacceptable contexts.

There are two major differences in methodology that are candidates for being the cause of the conflict. First, Stanovich and West employed a naming task in their experiments while Fischler and Bloom employed a lexical decision task, and secondly, the neutral condition was different in the two research programmes. Forster (1981) undertook a study that examined which of these two factors, if either, was the cause of the empirical conflict.

It would not be surprising if it were found that the task difference was an important factor. An attentional decision strategy would seem to be far less relevant to a naming response than a lexical decision response: Being biased towards thinking that a target is a word or not would be more likely to have an effect on a "Yes/No" decision than on a decision as to whether or not the appropriate word is being pronounced. However, it seems that the difference in tasks is not the explanation. When Forster compared naming responses to lexical decision responses using the same set of items, he found that both tasks revealed a significant inhibition effect for incongruous targets and no facilitation for congruous unpredictable targets. In other words, Forster replicated Fischler and Bloom's results with naming as well as with lexical decision. Interestingly, though, Forster found a significant facilitation effect for highly predictable targets in the lexical decision task only, not in the naming task. Such a result is diametrically opposed to that obtained by Stanovich and West who found a significant facilitation effect on naming times not only when the congruous target was highly predictable, but even when it was not predictable. Before turning to Forster's interpretation of his data, we must consider the second factor that may have led to Stanovich and West producing a different pattern of results to those that others have obtained. This concerns the nature of the neutral condition.

The Importance of the Baseline

A variety of neutral contexts have been used as a baseline for determining the amount of facilitation or inhibition arising from the sentential context. For example, Schuberth and Eimas (1977) employed a blank field, Stanovich and West (1981), and West and Stanovich (1982) used a non-specific sentence fragment like THEY SAID IT WAS THE, Fischler and Bloom (1979) employed a row of X's, and Forster (1981) chose a list of unrelated words.

Clearly, it is very important for the neutral condition to be an appropriate baseline, since the existence of facilitation or inhibition is predicated upon this assumption. It is possible, for example, that the failure of Stanovich and West to obtain an inhibition effect, while at the same time finding a facilitation effect for congruent unpredictable targets, could have arisen from the use of a neutral condition that overestimated the baseline, being associated with relatively slow response times. Support for this view comes from Forster (1981). He simply examined naming performance on the items used by Stanovich and West (1981), comparing the pattern of results obtained when the neutral context consisted of the non-specific sentence fragments used by Stanovich and West with the pattern of results obtained when the neutral context consisted of a random word list. What Forster found was a significant facilitation effect for congruous targets and no significant inhibition effect for incongruous targets when the non-specific sentence fragments were used (i.e. "facilitation dominant" data), and vice versa when the random word lists were used (i.e. "inhibition dominant" data). In other words, Stanovich and West's results were replicated when using their own neutral condition, while Fischler and Bloom's results were replicated using a word list as the neutral condition.

It might be argued, however, that it was not that Stanovich and West overestimated the baseline by using an inappropriate neutral condition, but rather, that Forster as well as Fischler and Bloom actually underestimated the baseline. There is, however, evidence to suggest otherwise. In both the Forster and the Fischler and Bloom studies, responses to nonwords were not facilitated in a sentential context relative to the neutral context, whereas in a study by West and Stanovich (1982), they were. Now, according to the dual-process model, facilitation effects for nonword targets occur as a result of the same attentional decision bias that leads to inhibition for incongruous targets. Therefore, it should not be possible to find either of these two effects in the absence of the other. Yet, both Forster and Fischler and Bloom obtain inhibition effects in lexical decision while at the same time finding no nonword facilitation, and West and Stanovich (1982) obtain a facilitation effect for nonwords while finding no inhibition effect for incongruous targets. What this means is that a nonword facilitation effect is difficult to explain theoretically and suggests that, if it occurs, responses to the neutral condition are taking longer than they should. In other words, it seems that in the Stanovich and West studies, the neutral condition was overestimating the baseline and that therefore one can conclude that there is actually no facilitation for words which are congruent but not predictable in the context. Indeed, Kinoshita, Taft, and Taplin (1985) found that by manipulating the existence of a facilitation effect for nonword items, one could alter the pattern of facilitation and inhibition on the word items. When nonword facilitation was generated, the data were facilitation dominant, whereas when nonword facilitation was eliminated, the data were inhibition dominant.

It seems then that the results that need to be explained by any theory of sentence processing are those found when the appropriate baseline is used, namely, an inhibition effect for inappropriate target words and no facilitation effect for unpredictable but appropriate target words in both a lexical decision and a naming task (Fischler & Bloom, 1979; Forster, 1981; Kinoshita et al., 1985). In addition, one's theory needs to account for the fact that responses to highly predictable words are facilitated only when they are lexical decision responses, and not when they are naming responses (Forster, 1981). In other words, the system seems to be set up primarily to inhibit words that are inappropriate to the context, rather than to facilitate words that are congruous with the context. How and why might this be so?

A Post-access Inhibitory Mechanism

Forster (1981) puts forward a contextual mechanism that plays its part after a lexical entry has been accessed on the basis of sensory information. Once the lexical entry for a word is accessed, an attempt is made to integrate that word into the sentential context. When the word cannot be readily integrated with the context, the response to that word, be it lexical decision or naming, will be delayed and hence, inhibition effects will be observed. There is no reason to suppose that being able to integrate a word into the context will be any faster than not having any sentential context at all, and therefore there is no reason to expect facilitation effects. The facilitation effect that is observed for highly predictable targets in the lexical decision task, arises from a decision stage that is specific to that task, namely, when a word that can be guessed from the context actually is the one that is accessed, one can be confident that a "Yes" response is the correct response.

That the inhibitory effect arises from post-access mechanisms has also been claimed by Mitchell and Green (1978), Kinoshita et al. (1985), and Norris (1986). In addition, it is consistent with the findings of Schuberth, Spoehr, and Lane (1981), who observed that inhibition was unaffected by stimulus degradation or by word frequency and therefore appears to arise after these factors have played their role, namely, after lexical access (although it should be noted that these results are in conflict with those obtained by Stanovich & West, 1979).

Kinoshita et al. and Norris propose that the delay that arises when a word cannot be integrated with the rest of the sentence comes about because, prior to making the response, consideration is given to other candidate entries which are less congruent with the incoming sensory information. The reason for the system being set up in this way is so that it can handle a situation where the sensory information has led to the wrong lexical entry being accessed. This can happen when the word has been misperceived, or when there is a typographical error, or when the word is ambiguous. In such circumstances, it is important to be able to make use of the context to determine what word was really intended.

Research into the processing of ambiguous words has indeed supported the view that context plays its part by helping to select the intended meaning from those candidates which have been accessed on the basis of sensory information (e.g. Kinoshita, 1985; Onifer & Swinney, 1981; Seidenberg, Tanenhaus, Leiman, & Bienkowski, 1982; Swinney, 1979; Tanenhaus, Leiman, & Seidenberg, 1979). We turn now to the issue of how words with more than one meaning are accessed.

ACCESSING AMBIGUOUS WORDS

The Ambiguous Word in Context

It is apparent that the two meanings of an ambiguous word are accessed in order of frequency, with the dominant meaning (e.g. the "leather strap" meaning of BELT) being accessed prior to the subordinate meaning (e.g. the "hit" meaning of BELT). Forster and Bednall (1976), for example, found that response times to say that THE BELT was a grammatical phrase were faster than those to say that TO BELT was. Hogaboam and Perfetti (1975) placed ambiguous words at the end of sentences which biased the interpretation of the ambiguous words either toward their dominant meaning (e.g. YOUR TROUSERS WILL FALL DOWN WITHOUT A BELT) or toward their subordinate meaning (e.g. THAT'S THE NAUGHTY BOY I WOULD LOVE TO BELT). When asked whether the last word was ambiguous or not, subjects were faster to respond in the subordinate bias condition. This suggests that the dominant meaning was rapidly accessed even when the context favoured the subordinate meaning, while the subordinate meaning took some time to access when the context favoured the dominant meaning.

While one meaning may take longer to access than another, is it the case that the sentential context of a word can narrow the focus of processing down to a single meaning prior to access? The post-access contextual mechanism supported in the previous section would suggest not. Studies which have employed a semantic priming paradigm have indeed indicated that both meanings of an ambiguous word are typically accessed when that word is presented for recognition. For example, Holley-Wilcox and Blank (1980) found that the presence of an ambiguous word, like BANK, facilitated subsequent lexical decision responses to target words related to either of the two meanings, like RIVER or MONEY, suggesting that both meanings are accessed. Schvaneveldt, Meyer, & Becker (1976) demonstrated that a prior single-word context can bias processing towards one meaning only, in that RIVER was no longer facilitated by the prior presentation of BANK when BANK was preceded by MONEY. When the biasing context is a sentence, however, it seems that both meanings of the polysemous word are accessed. This has been demonstrated using the semantic priming paradigm (e.g. Conrad, 1974; Oden & Spira, 1983; Onifer & Swinney, 1981; Seidenberg et al., 1982; Swinney, 1979; Tanenhaus et al., 1979) whereby, for example, responses to both RIVER and MONEY are influenced by the prior presentation of SHE DEPOSITED HER SAVINGS IN THE BANK.

In addition, it has been demonstrated in a variety of tasks that the presence of a polysemous word in a sentence slows down the processing of that sentence (e.g. Cairns & Kamerman, 1975; Carpenter & Daneman, 1981; Foss, 1970; Holmes, 1979) suggesting that both meanings of an ambiguous word are accessed despite the fact that one meaning might be more common than the other and that the context is only appropriate to one of the meanings. It does seem, however, that the difficulty in processing decreases the more the context is biased towards one of the two meanings (e.g. Holmes, 1979; Carpenter & Daneman, 1981).

The research that suggests that both meanings of an ambiguous word are accessed when placed in a context which is appropriate to only one of the meanings, supports the post-access inhibitory account of context effects. According to this view, ambiguity resolution comes about when the context allows all but one of the meanings of a polysemous word to be suppressed after they have been accessed. On the other hand, a pre-access account might be seen to be supported by the fact that when the context is strongly biased towards one of the meanings of a polysemous word, the response to that word seems to reflect the influence of only the appropriate meaning. According to this pre-access account, the context serves to focus the access mechanism on to appropriate meanings only and, therefore, inappropriate meanings are not accessed at all.

Cross-modal Priming

Just because context is seen to resolve ambiguity, however, does not mean that the inappropriate meanings are not accessed at all. Even according to the post-access account, context does eventually bias the response to the appropriate meaning only. The crucial concern of any experiment that demonstrates ambiguity resolution should be the point in the sentence at which the contextual bias has its effects. A task is needed which gauges lexical processing at the actual point of ambiguity to determine whether or not all the meanings of the ambiguous word are accessed. One task which has been employed with this in mind is cross-modal priming whereby a letter string is visually presented at the same time that an ambiguous word is heard within a spoken sentence. Subjects are required to make a lexical decision response to the letter string, which, when it forms a word, is either semantically related or unrelated to the spoken ambiguous word.

Swinney (1979), Tanenhaus et al. (1979), Onifer and Swinney (1981), Seidenberg et al. (1982), and Lucas (1987) have all used the cross-modal priming technique to reveal a priming effect for both meanings of the polysemous word, despite the fact that one of the meanings is more common than the other and despite the fact that the context was heavily biased in favour of one of the meanings. For example, in the experiment of Onifer and Swinney, subjects heard sentences like ALL THE CASH THAT WAS KEPT IN THE SAFE AT THE BANK WAS STOLEN LAST WEEK. At the point when the ambiguous word BANK was heard, subjects were visually presented with MONEY, RIVER, or an unrelated word like STUDY, and were required to make a lexical decision response. What Onifer and Swinney found were faster lexical decision responses to both MONEY and RIVER compared to STUDY. In addition, when the visual presentation of the target word was delayed until 1.5 seconds after the offset of the spoken ambiguous word, facilitation was only observed for the relevant target, MONEY. Response times to RIVER were no longer faster than those to STUDY. In other words, even though the "river" meaning of BANK was not appropriate to the context and, furthermore, is less frequent than the "money" meaning, it still seemed to be accessed at the point when BANK was being processed. Subsequently, the context was used to select from the accessed meanings and hence only the relevant meaning was available to influence the lexical decision response.

The cross-modal priming technique has therefore been able to reveal that context is not typically used to select potential lexical candidates prior to access, but rather is used to select amongst the multiple candidates that have been accessed.

Backward Priming

While the results of the cross-modal priming experiments seem to favour a post-access locus for the influence of context on lexical processing, they have not been immune from criticism. Glucksberg, Kreuz, and Rho (1986) have argued that the results observed at zero second delay favouring multiple access of meanings, could have arisen from the artefact of "backward priming" (Koriat, 1981; Kiger & Glass, 1983). The spoken prime (e.g. BANK) is still being processed when the visual target (e.g. RIVER, MONEY, or STUDY) is presented, and Glucksberg et al. (1986) suggest that the meaning of the visual target therefore has time to bias the interpretation of the ambiguous prime. In this way, either the "river" or the "money" interpretation of the word BANK will be accessed depending upon which visual target is presented. The spoken prime word, disambiguated by the visual target, in turn facilitates the decision that the visual target is a word, thus priming both RIVER and MONEY. Note that for this argument to make sense, it must be possible for meaning to be extracted from the visual target and used to disambiguate the spoken prime word prior to there being enough evidence to say that the target is actually a word. The "cascade model" put forward by McClelland (1979) is one such model which incorporates the notion that processing at one level (e.g. orthographic) need not be completed before information is extracted at a higher level (e.g. semantic).

Glucksberg et al. (1986) present indirect support for their view that the apparent evidence for multiple access can be explained by backward priming. They claim that if one presents an ambiguous word followed by a target nonword, lexical decision responses to that nonword will be delayed if it resembles a word which is associatively related to either meaning of the ambiguous word (e.g. BANK RIVEB and BANK MONAY take longer than BEAT RIVEB and BEAT MONAY respectively). On the other hand, when Glucksberg et al. presented the ambiguous word in a spoken sentence with the nonword as a simultaneous visual target, lexical decisions to the nonword were delayed only when it resembled a word associatively related to the one meaning of the ambiguous word that was appropriate to the sentence (e.g. MONAY, but not RIVEB, when the sentence was THE YOUNG COUPLE PUT ALL THEIR SAVINGS INTO THEIR BANK ACCOUNT). In other words, the context appeared to have already disambiguated the ambiguous word at the point when that word was being processed, which is the opposite conclusion to that arising from the cross-modal priming studies using words as targets. The possibility of backward priming was obviated in this experiment since nonwords do not show any effects of backward priming. That is, BANK is neither facilitated nor inhibited by the prior presentation of RIVEB or MONAY. Hence, Glucksberg et al. concluded that the only cross-modal priming results that are acceptable are those obtained with nonword targets, and that those obtained with word targets are contaminated by backward priming.

These conclusions have been challenged by Burgess, Tanenhaus, and Seidenberg (1989). What they suggest is that the sentence context could have affected the post-lexical decision that the target was a nonword. When the nonword MONAY, for example, is presented it accesses the lexical entry for MONEY, and it is during the evaluation of whether this lexical entry represents the actual target item that the contextual information plays its role. If the accessed lexical entry is compatible with the context, there is a bias toward thinking that it does represent the target stimulus and hence that the target stimulus is a word. In this way, only the contextually appropriate nonword will incur a delay, and this has nothing to do with the fact that the sentence contains an ambiguous word at all. Burgess et al. (1989) support their argument by replacing the ambiguous words with unambiguous words (e.g. THE YOUNG COUPLE PUT ALL THEIR SAVINGS INTO THEIR NEW HOUSE rather than THE YOUNG COUPLE PUT ALL THEIR SAVINGS INTO THEIR BANK ACCOUNT) and produced the same pattern of results as that obtained by Glucksberg et al. (i.e. a delay in responding to MONAY compared to RIVEB). Therefore, the results used by Glucksberg et al. to support their backward priming position have an alternative explanation. However, the study by Burgess et al. does not directly counter the possibility that the cross-modal priming effects with words as targets are contaminated by backward priming; but, neither does the study by Glucksberg et al. directly demonstrate the existence of any such contamination.

Tabossi (1988) presents clear evidence against the idea that backward priming was the cause of the findings which supported the access of multiple meanings. By varying the content of the sentential context prior to the ambiguous word, but holding the presentation conditions constant, Tabossi was able to produce two different patterns of results. When the context emphasized a salient feature of the dominant meaning of the ambiguous word the results favoured the selective access position (i.e. only the target related to the contextually appropriate meaning was primed), whereas when the sentential context was not highly constraining the results favoured the multiple access position (i.e. a target related to any of the word's meanings were primed). The backward priming argument can no longer be invoked to explain the finding of equal priming for both meanings of the ambiguous word at zero second delay, since the selective access pattern of results was also able to be obtained under these same presentation conditions. However, the fact that it is possible to find evidence for selective access at zero second delay is in itself a problem for the view that context only plays its role after access has taken place.

Simpson (1981) was also able to generate results favouring selective access when the context was strongly biasing toward one meaning of the ambiguous word. However, there was a 120msec delay between the offset of the ambiguous word and the onset of the target, during which time post-access disambiguation could have taken place. In order to maintain the view that multiple access always occurs followed by a post-access selection of meaning (e.g. Onifer & Swinney), one would need to maintain that there was also sufficient delay between the prime and target in the Tabossi (1988) study for a strongly biasing context to select amongst the several meanings which had been accessed. Since the timing used by Tabossi was the same as that used by Onifer and Swinney, such an argument is hard to sustain. Both used a zero second delay between the offset of the spoken word and the onset of the visual target. One possibility, however, is that there is a difference in the timing of recognizing spoken English words and spoken Italian words (as used by Tabossi). It may be the case that the identification of an Italian word (or at least its stem) can be made prior to the offset of the word to a greater extent than in English, since Italian words always have an inflectional suffix. For example, the Italian word for PORT is PORTO which has an extra syllable following its stem morpheme. If the two meanings of PORTO are already available once the stem PORT- is processed, then there is time for selection of the appropriate meaning to take place while the -O is being uttered, notably when the context is so strong that the appropriate meaning is easily selected.

If it turns out though that Tabossi's results cannot be explained in this way, we are left with the conclusion that context does occasionally bias lexical access, but mostly does not. What sort of model would allow this sort of flexibility?

Interactive-Activation

According to McClelland (1987), the interactive-activation model is able to explain the cross-modal priming data. When the spoken ambiguous word is presented, both meanings become activated. At the same time, however, information which has already been extracted at the higher sentential levels is fed back to the lower lexical level in order to inhibit the activation of words which are inappropriate to the context and to further activate words which are appropriate to the context. Some time is required before this feedback has any observable impact, although the stronger the contextual constraint the earlier will be its impact. The basic difference between this model and the multiple access position lies in the timing of the effect of the context. In the multiple access model, the various meanings of the word are all accessed before the contextual checking mechanism comes into play, whereas in the interactive-activation model, the context influences the activation of the various meanings of the word while those meanings are in the process of being activated.

According to the multiple access model, it would not be surprising if contextual checking were brought into play before any very unusual meanings of the word had been accessed. However, unlike the interactive-activation model, the strength of contextual constraint should have no impact on the time at which the context is brought into play. One could say, however, that the stronger the contextual constraint the more readily the appropriate candidate can be selected from amongst the alternatives. Therefore, according to the multiple access model, it is possible for the strength of contextual constraint to influence whether one or both of the meanings are available, although importantly, not at zero second delay where both meanings should be active. It is for this reason that Tabossi's findings are more compatible with the interactive-activation position than the multiple access position, since they appear to demonstrate that only one meaning is available when the context is sufficiently constraining even at zero second delay between prime and target.

Furthermore, McClelland (1987) points out that of the six reported experiments which demonstrate that targets related to either meaning of the spoken prime word are facilitated at zero second delay, five experiments show a tendency for the context-appropriate meaning to be more facilitative than the context-inappropriate meaning, although never significantly. Thus, McClelland wants to say that context has at least began to play some role in disambiguating the meaning of an ambiguous word at the earliest stages of the processing of that word, just as the interactive-activation model predicts. However, such a conclusion must be tempered by the fact that five out of six experiments showing the same pattern of effects is not significantly greater than chance according to binomial probabilities (particularly since the experiments were not always completely independent in terms of materials).

Therefore, all one can say is that the evidence used to support the multiple access view is compatible with an interactive-activation view, where the contextual information has a delayed effect on the disambiguation of the ambiguous word. If no other explanation can be found for Tabossi's results, however, the interactive-activation account would be favoured. Note, however, that the interactive-activation account being referred to here is one where there is a sentential level which sends activation down to the word level. This is not, however, a necessary feature of the model. It is possible to have an interactive-activation system which extends only as far as the word level, and that context has its effects in the post-access inhibitory manner described in this chapter.

One final point worth noting about the research conducted on ambiguous word processing is that much of it, in particular the cross-modal priming studies, is actually examining lexical processing in speech comprehension rather than in reading. Although the cross-modal studies require a response to a visually presented word, the lexical processing that is of central interest is that of the spoken ambiguous word. We must be cautious about generalizing the conclusions drawn from these studies to the reading situation, since it may be the case that context is a more important factor in auditory lexical processing than visual lexical processing (see, for example, Marslen-Wilson & Tyler, 1980). An auditory signal is very likely to be less intelligible at the sensory level than is a visual stimulus and, hence, may require more contextual input for it to be interpreted. Given this likelihood, the results of Onifer and Swinney and others are all the more impressive, since they demonstrate that the several meanings of an ambiguous word are typically accessed, not only in the face of a contextual bias in favour of only one meaning, but also in the face of presentation conditions which should optimize the influence of context.

SYNTACTIC CONTEXTS

So far the discussion of the influence of context on lexical processing has focused upon semantic factors. However, the context in which a word occurs provides syntactic as well as semantic constraints and, therefore, it is worth considering whether these have any effect upon lexical processing.

Two-word Phrases

Goodman, McClelland, and Gibbs (1981) were the first to demonstrate an effect of syntactic structure on lexical processing. They examined two-word phrases, observing a difference in lexical decision times to a target word when it was preceded by a syntactically congruent word compared to when it was preceded by a syntactically incongruent word. For example, responses to the word AGREED were faster when preceded by WE than when preceded by NO. Lukatela, Kostic, Feldman, and Turvey (1983) obtained a similar result using prepositions and inflected nouns in Serbo-Croatian. Such syntactic priming was also observed by Seidenberg et al. (1984a), but only for lexical decision responses and not for naming responses. They therefore concluded that the syntactic priming effect arose at a post-access decision phase specific to the lexical decision task. This contrasts with the single-word semantic priming described earlier, which is observed in both the lexical decision and naming task, and is therefore attributed to spreading activation.

The conclusions regarding semantic priming are, however, based upon the fact that a target which is semantically congruent with the prime is responded to more quickly, in both the lexical decision and naming task, than a target preceded by a row of X's. The inhibitory effect on a target preceded by a semantically incongruent prime was only observed in the lexical decision task (Forster, 1981; Lorch et al., 1986), and this is compatible with the interpretation of the inhibitory effect arising from a post-access decision phase. It may well be the case that the syntactic priming effect is actually an inhibitory effect and that is why it is eliminated in the naming task.

In support of this, Goodman et al. found that lexical decision responses to a neutral condition (e.g. XX AGREED) were no different from those to the congruent condition (e.g. WE AGREED), but were faster than those to the incongruent condition (e.g. NO AGREED). Therefore, it is possible to conclude that the only effect that syntactic context has on lexical processing, at least within two-word phrases, is an inhibitory one (for syntactically incorrect phrases) arising at a post-access decision stage.

Sentential Syntactic Context

When it comes to sentential contexts, the effect of syntactic structure on lexical decisions has been shown to be very robust. Wright and Garrett (1984) observed that target words which continued in a syntactically correct manner from a given sentence context were consistently associated with shorter lexical decision responses than those which did not. For example, with a preceding context of THE AMERICAN POLITICAL SYSTEM CAN, lexical decision times for the target word LOCATE were faster than for the target word ERRORS, but vice versa when the preceding context was THE FORMER GENERAL CONCLUDED WITH. A verb (like LOCATE) grammatically follows a modal (like CAN), but not a preposition (like WITH), whereas a noun (like ERRORS) follows a preposition, but not a modal. The fact that none of the targets created a meaningful sentence, eliminated any semantic explanation for the result.

West and Stanovich (1986) replicated this finding and extended it by demostrating that the effect was an inhibitory one rather than a facilitatory one. They found no difference in response times between targets which followed grammatically from the context and those which followed a neutral sentence frame (THE NEXT WORD WILL BE), while targets which did not follow grammatically from the context were responded to more slowly. Since the effect appeared to be purely inhibitory in nature, one might expect that the effect would disappear in a naming task given the logic that inhibition arises from a post-access decision stage that is more relevant to lexical decision than to naming. This was not the case, however. West and Stanovich obtained an inhibitory effect (and no facilitatory effect) in a naming task as well as in the lexical decision task. From this they concluded that the syntactic influence on lexical processing is indeed post-lexical, given its inhibitory nature, but that the naming response is sensitive to these syntactic post-lexical effects. They suggest that the post-lexical stage being affected by syntactic factors might be a stage where the lexical information about the word's pronunciation is edited prior to its articulation. Syntactically inappropriate words might be inhibited at this stage, but why this should be so is not made clear.

CONCLUSION

In this chapter we have seen that it can be argued that the processes involved in accessing a word in the lexicon are not affected by the semantic and syntactic characteristics of either the word itself or the preceding sentential context. Lexical access does not appear to be fundamentally different when the word is contained in a sentence context compared to when it is presented in isolation. It seems that the primary effect of sentential context, both at the semantic and syntactic levels, is to influence post-access decision mechanisms, and in particular, to inhibit any inappropriate candidates that have been accessed (or are in the process of being accessed). It may be the case that such mechanisms are unique to the artificial task of lexical decision and hence say little about the reading process itself; but it may also be the case that such inhibitory mechanisms are an important part of the reading process in that they facilitate acceptance of the appropriate lexical entry by suppressing any other lexical entries that have been inappropriately accessed, or, according to an interactive-activation account, are in the process of being accessed.

Given then that the decoding mechanisms involved in accessing words in context are essentially the same as those involved in accessing isolated words, the remaining chapters will focus on research which examines the nature of those decoding mechanisms, using isolated letter strings as stimuli.

NOTE

1. See Ratcliff and McKoon (1988) for an alternative to spreading activation, namely, compound cue theory.

CHAPTER FOUR

Phonological Recoding

Children learn to use language in its spoken form prior to learning it in its printed form, so that when they learn to read they already have a phonologically accessible lexicon. It has consequently been supposed that learning to read is simply a matter of translating the printed word into its phonological form so that the already extant lexicon can be accessed. Further, and more controversially, it has been supposed that proficient adult reading is typically achieved via this route as well (e.g. Gibson, 1970; Gough, 1972; Klapp, 1971; H. Rubenstein et al., 1971a). In seeming agreement with this idea is the experience of "hearing" a voice inside one's head while reading, and also the finding that electromyographic recordings from the articulatory mechanisms (lips, larynx, etc.) demonstrate activity during silent reading (e.g. Hardyck & Petrinovich, 1970 ; McGuigan, 1970).

For printed words to be translated into a phonological form prior to lexical access, there must exist a set of rules which translate graphemes (i.e. letters or letter groupings) into phonemes (i.e. sounds). Venezky (1970) provides a description of what such grapheme-to-phoneme conversion (GPC) rules might be like; for example, C is pronounced /s/ when followed by E, I, or Y. One could suppose (as does M. Coltheart, 1980) that GPC rules must necessarily exist since readers are able to consistently pronounce nonsense words which they have never heard pronounced before (e.g. CLIMP → /klɪmp/). We shall see, however, that there is an alternative way in which nonwords could be pronounced without recourse to rules. In addition though, it cannot be the case that GPC rules are always used in determining the phonological form of a word, since the relationship between graphemes and phonemes in English is highly variable. For example, the pronunciation of OUGH is different in the words COUGH, THROUGH, ENOUGH, and DOUGH, while the letter O has a different pronunciation in the words DOG, WOMAN, WOMEN, SON, TOLL, and TOMB.

Nevertheless, despite the fact that the pronunciation of irregular words cannot be determined by means of GPC rules, there have been experiments carried out which have been put forward as supporting the notion that a phonological route is used in the recognition of visually presented words.

HOMOPHONY AND PSEUDOHOMOPHONY

Rubenstein, Lewis, and Rubenstein

H. Rubenstein et al. (1971a) reasoned that if words are phonologically recoded, there should be some difficulty in recognizing a word which is pronounced in the same way as another differently spelt word (i.e. a homophone like WEAK which is pronounced identically to WEEK). Using the same logic as that outlined in Chapter 2 when describing the word similarity effect, there should be a delay in lexical decision responses when an inappropriate lexical entry is accessed. H. Rubenstein et al. adopted a search-like model. If WEAK is recoded into its phonological form /wi:k/, and access is then attempted using the phonological input system, then the most common word which is represented as /wi:k/ will be accessed. Since WEEK is the most common word represented as /wi:k/, it will be the first word to be accessed and will only be found to be inappropriate when a post-access check, using the accessed orthographic information about the word, revealed that WEEK was not the word that was presented. Confirming this expectation, H. Rubenstein et al. reported a delay in lexical decision responses to homophones (like WEAK) compared to non-homophones which were matched on frequency (like CLAY).

In another experiment, H. Rubenstein et al. reported a word similarity effect with nonwords which were homophonic with real words (e.g. an item like LEEF took longer to classify as a nonword than an item like NEEF). This finding has become known as the "pseudohomophone effect" and the interpretation of it is similar to that outlined above for word items. LEEF accesses the phonological representation of the word LEAF after being recoded as /li:f/, and thus an inappropriate lexical entry is accessed, whereas NEEF is recoded as /ni:f/ which cannot be found in the phonological input system.

The finding by H. Rubenstein et al. that homophony and pseudohomophony lead to a delay in lexical decision times, appears to provide strong support for the idea that words are accessed after they have been phonologically recoded. However, a critical appraisal by Clark (1973) of the statistical analyses carried out in these studies suggested that the homophone effect observed with word items should not be viewed as a genuine effect, since it cannot be generalized beyond the items used in that particular experiment. The pseudohomophone effect, on the other hand, did hold up to statistical re-analysis.

The Dual-route Model

Consistent with Clark's conclusions, M. Coltheart et al. (1977) failed to find a homophone effect for word items in a lexical decision task, but did observe a clear pseudohomophone effect (as did Patterson & Marcel, 1977; Besner & Davelaar, 1983; and Dennis, Besner, & Davelaar, 1985, amongst others). On the basis of these findings, M. Coltheart et al. support a dual-route model of lexical access (see also M. Coltheart, 1978, 1980). This view holds that there is both a direct visual route to the lexicon and an indirect phonological route mediated by GPC rules. Both routes are followed when a word is to be read, but the direct visual route is typically faster. The phonological route, therefore, only influences processing when the visual route is very slow or fails to locate an appropriate entry. Since this will be the case when a nonword is presented, phonological effects should manifest themselves in lexical decisions to nonwords, but not to words (except perhaps for very low frequency words for which the direct visual route will take a long time).[1] Hence the dual-route model neatly accounts for the general absence of a homophone effect despite the existence of a pseudohomophone effect.

However, in order to accept the conclusion that the pseudohomophone effect reflects the use of a secondary phonological route to the lexicon, it must be established that the effect is genuinely a result of phonological factors. It is actually possible that the effect arises from orthographic factors. Taking the example of LEEF versus NEEF; the former item is not only pronounced in exactly the same way as the word LEAF, but is also orthographically very similar to LEAF, while NEEF is not similar to any word. M. Coltheart et al. (1977) attempted to control for the orthographic similarity of their nonwords to real words by changing only a single letter of each pseudohomophonic item to produce each nonhomophonic item. Yet this technique is ineffective as a control for orthographic similarity as we see in the example of LEEF and NEEF, which differ from each other by one letter, but which also differ on their similarity to a real word. In order to be sure that homophony and orthographic similarity are not confounded, one must use pseudohomophones and nonhomophones which are matched exactly on their similarity to real words.

Orthographic Similarity Effects

R.C. Martin (1982) controlled for orthographic similarity by making the same letter change in creating nonhomophones from words as was made in creating pseudohomophones from words. For example, the nonhomophone PESH is created from PUSH by changing the U to an E, just as the pseudohomophone HERT is created from HURT. A similar procedure was followed by Taft (1982), although here, the letter change occurred in the same letter environment. For example, the nonhomophone DEEF was matched with the pseudohomophone LEEF, where the former is as orthographically similar to DEAF as the latter is to LEAF.

In both the Martin and Taft studies there was no difference found between the lexical decision responses to the pseudohomophones (like HERT and LEEF), and those to the orthographically similar nonhomophones (like PESH and DEEF), while both were more difficult to classify as nonwords than orthographically distinct nonhomophones (like ZERT and NEEF). Such a result implies that the pseudohomophone effect need not be interpreted as a phonological effect since the orthographic similarity of the pseudohomophone to its source word is sufficient to explain the delay in response times, and therefore the evidence provided for the idea of a phonological "back-up" route to the lexicon is undermined.

Taft (1982) went on to specify what was meant by orthographic similarity in this context. Rather than defining orthographic similarity simply in terms of the number of letters in common, Taft put forward the notion of rule-governed orthographic similarity whereby two graphemic units are seen to be similar if they can be pronounced in the same way. For example, the pronunciation of the graphemic units EA and EE is typically the same, and therefore these two units have a relationship that EA does not have with OA. Thus DEAF and DEEF are more orthographically similar to each other than DEAF and DOAF. Taft characterizes this relationship by suggesting that there exist grapheme-to-grapheme conversion (GGC) rules that are used instead of grapheme-to-phoneme conversion rules, for example, EA ↔ EE rather than EA → /i:/ and EE → /i:/. Thus DEEF is related to DEAF by the above grapheme-to-grapheme rule (just as LEEF is related to LEAF, by the same rule). The sort of evidence that Taft presents to support his position is the following.

The letter string CHALC would be converted into the word CHALK if GGC rules were applied to it, since C ↔ K would be such a rule. HALC, on the other hand, would not become a word via the application of such rules since HALK is not a word. Nonwords like CHALC were found by Taft to take longer to classify in a lexical decision task than nonwords like HALC, thus supporting the rule-governed graphemic similarity view. This result cannot be explained in terms of grapheme-to-phoneme recoding since the phonological recoding of HALC would be just as similar to the pronunciation of the word HAWK as the phonological recoding of CHALC would be to CHALK. Similarly, an explanation cannot be made in terms of the general visual similarity of CHALC to CHALK since HALC is also only one letter different from a real word (e.g. HALO and HALF). Hence it seems that the only reason for response times to be slower to CHALC than to HALC is the special relationship that exists between the letters C and K that leads to confusion between CHALC and CHALK.

An experiment by Besner, Dennis, and Davelaar (1985), however, has cast doubt on the notion of GGC rules and the conclusion that the pseudohomophone effect is merely the result of orthographic similarity. What their study demonstrated was that a word is primed by the prior presentation of a homophonic nonword (e.g. lexical decision times to LEAF were found to be faster when preceded by LEEF than when preceded by an unrelated nonword like ZERT), while a word is not primed by the prior presentation of an orthographically similar nonword (e.g. lexical decision times to DEAF were found to be no faster when preceded by DEEF than when preceded by ZERT). If GGC rules were applied to both DEEF and LEEF, they should have produced priming effects of equivalent size. However, there appears to be another way of accounting for the results obtained by Besner et al. (1985).

Grapheme-to-grapheme conversion rules were originally defined as rules by which one can interchange graphemes that can be pronounced identically. However, we can sensibly qualify this definition by saying that graphemes are only interchangeable if they are pronounced identically in the same letter environment. For example, a rule that says that C interchanges with S must specify that this is only true when followed by an E, I, or Y, since in other environments the two consonants are never pronounced identically (cf. CELL and SELL, CYMBAL and SYMBOL as opposed to CAT and SAT, CLAM and SLAM). Now, if this qualified version of grapheme-to-grapheme conversion is used to define orthographic similarity, then 13 of the 40 item pairs which Besner et al. considered to be related by GGC rules, are not in fact related in this way (e.g. SART and CART, GROB and GRAB, JUN and GUN). It is possible therefore, that Besner et al. obtained no significant priming effect with grapheme-to-grapheme related items because they did not always use appropriate GGC rules. An unpublished study in the author's laboratory by G. Cruchley and I. Merhav did find that grapheme-to-grapheme related items produced as much priming as homophonically related items when using the more rigorous definition of GGC rules.

So we see that the existence of a pseudohomophone effect cannot necessarily be taken as support for the use of an indirect phonological route to the lexicon, since it could be accounted for in orthographic terms.

A result that seemingly conflicts with this conclusion, however, is the finding that lexical decision times to pseudohomophones can be differentiated from those to orthographically matched controls under certain conditions, namely when homophonic words are included in the experiment (Dennis et al., 1985; Underwood, Roberts, & Thomason, 1988). Thus it seems that phonological factors are indeed involved in the pseudohomophone effect. However, Dennis et al. and Underwood et al. used orthographic controls of the sort that R.C. Martin (1982) used (e.g. PESH based on PUSH, versus HERT based on HURT) and therefore these control nonwords were not related to their base words in terms of context sensitive grapheme-to-grapheme rules (e.g. while there would be a rule ER ↔ UR, there would not be a rule E ↔ U). Therefore, it could be argued that when there are no homophones present, the only effects observed are those arising from gross visual similarity to a word (which is the same for pseudohomophones and their matched controls), whereas the presence of homophones induces the use of grapheme-to-grapheme rules which increases the processing time for pseudohomophones relative to nonhomophones. Therefore, a possible orthographic explanation for the pseudohomophone effect still remains.

Homophone Decision

M. Coltheart (1980) uses a common-sense argument in relation to homophony to support the position that an indirect phonological route to the lexicon must at least exist. He points out that people can readily say that a pseudohomophone like SKREAM is pronounced like a real word and claims that such a task can only be carried out by recoding the nonword into its phonological form (i.e. /skri:m/) and then accessing the word SCREAM through the phonological input system (i.e. via the indirect phonological route to the lexicon).

If this is the way in which such a homophony decision is made, then the only orthographic characteristics of the nonword stimulus that should affect the speed of response should be the strength of the grapheme-to-phoneme relationship. For example, EA → /i:/ is more common than E-E → /iː/, and therefore it should be easier to say that SKREAM is homophonic with a word than to say the same of SKREME. Taft (1982), however, has demonstrated that it is not so much the strength of the grapheme-to-phoneme relationship that is important, but the orthographic similarity of the nonword to its homophonic word. So, while homophone decisions to SKREAM are indeed faster than those to SKREME, homophone decisions to SKEAM are slower than those to SKEME. What influences response times is the fact that SKREAM is orthographically more similar to SCREAM than is SKREME, and that SKEME is orthographically more similar to SCHEME than is SKEAM. This result means that the fact that we can decide that a letter string is homophonic with a real word cannot be used as unequivocal evidence for the existence of a phonological route to the lexicon, since such a route should be unaffected by orthographic similarity. The effect can, on the other hand, be explained using the notion of grapheme-to-grapheme conversion whereby the more similar the pseudohomophone is to the target word, the fewer the GGC rules required.

Further Studies of Homophony

If it turns out to be the case that the effects of homophony can be accounted for in terms of orthographic similarity rather than phonological identity, then doubt is cast on any study which purports to find an effect of homophony without controlling for rule-governed orthographic similarity. There are a number of studies looking at the effects of homophony in tasks other than lexical decision.

One such task requires subjects to decide whether a presented string of words is an acceptable sentence or not (e.g. Baron, 1973; Baron, Treiman, Freyd, & Kellman, 1980; V. Coltheart, Laxon, Rickard, & Elton, 1988; Treiman, Freyd, & Baron, 1983). In some instances, the sentence contains a word whose orthography makes the sentence unacceptable, but whose pronunciation is the same as a word which would make the sentence acceptable. For example, SHE HAS BLOND HARE is an orthographically unacceptable sentence, but is phonologically correct. Such sentences are found to either take longer to reject than control sentences like SHE HAS BLOND HARM (e.g. Treiman et al., 1983), or are wrongly accepted as correct sentences more often than control sentences (e.g. Baron, 1973). These results have been taken as support for the view that phonological recoding does occur, at least some of the time, in the reading of normal sentences.

These findings do not, however, necessitate the postulation of pre-lexical grapheme-to-phoneme conversion. It is possible, for example, that HARE is accessed on a visual basis and its pronunciation is then determined from stored lexical information. Difficulty in recognizing the acceptability of the sentence could then arise if this lexically generated pronunciation is held in working memory while the acceptability of the sentence is determined (e.g. Kleiman, 1975, and see later). An experiment by V. Coltheart et al. (1988) strongly supports this view. They simply demonstrated that the effect arises with irregular words just as it does with regular words. For example, more errors are made in classifying HE THROUGH OUT THE RUBBISH than in the control sentence SHE THOUGHT A BALL TO HIM. The pronunciation of THROUGH cannot be determined by rule and therefore the confusion between THROUGH and THREW must have arisen at a stage of processing after the pronunciation of the word had been extracted from the lexical entry.

Treiman et al. (1983), however, found a difference between regular and irregular words which would seem to favour the pre-access recoding position over this post-access account. When asked to read aloud sentences like THERE'S DUST IN THE ARE, subjects tended to regularize the pronunciation of the exception word (i.e. saying AIR instead of ARE) to a greater degree than when the sentence was acceptable, like I'M OLDER THAN YOU ARE. If pronunciations were being determined from lexical information rather than from rules, there is no reason for the pronunciation of ARE to ever be confused with the pronunciation of AIR, since the lexical entry for ARE would prescribe its specific pronunciation. Furthermore, Treiman et al. found that regular words were not "exceptionalized" when spoken in a sentence like I'M OLDER THAN YOU AIR (compared to control sentences like THERE'S DUST IN THE AIR). That is, AIR was rarely pronounced incorrectly as ARE. Such a pattern of results appears to support the use of pre-lexical phonological conversion, since it suggests that the interference only arises from inappropriate use of rules.

Importantly, however, the difference between the irregular words (as in THERE'S DUST IN THE ARE) and the regular words (as in I'M OLDER THAN YOU AIR) was essentially eradicated in an acceptability decision task, suggesting that pre-lexical rules only come into play during overt pronunciation.

It should be noted that an explanation for the results of the acceptability decision task could actually be given in terms of GGC rules rather than in terms of phonological factors. For example, use of the rule A-E ↔ AI would explain the confusion between HARE and HAIR and ARE and AIR. GGC rules could not, however, be used to explain the results obtained by Treiman et al. in the overt pronunciation task, since the grapheme-phoneme regularity of the word should be irrelevant, and therefore AIR should be mispronounced as often as ARE is. Such a conclusion is in the spirit of rule-governed orthographic similarity in that GGC rules provide a means of finding sensible approximations to inappropriately used letter strings without engaging the phonological system. Overt pronunciation necessarily engages the phonological system and therefore does not warrant the use of GGC rules.

Van Orden (1987) and Van Orden, Johnston, and Hale (1988) have come out in favour of pre-access phonological recoding on the basis of the results of a task which does not require overt pronunciation. Van Orden (1987) conducted several experiments using a semantic categorization task which demonstrated a greater number of false positive responses to words which were homophonic with a member of the category compared to those which were not. For example, BORE was mistakenly considered to be A WILD ANIMAL more often than was BORN.

Again, however, this result could be seen as arising from GGC rule application, for example, O-E ↔ OA. The further observation made by Van Orden that responses were influenced by the similarity of the spelling of the homophone to the real category exemplar is consistent with this position. The less similarly spelt homophones tended not to be misclassified, and for several of these items there is no obvious GGC rule linking them to their homophonic counterparts (e.g. SWEET and SUITE).

Against this though, is the finding that when the stimulus word was masked, the effect of orthographic similarity disappeared while the effect of homophony remained. If the effect of spelling similarity arose from GGC rule application, there is no reason for the homophony effect to actually increase for orthographically dissimilar items under masked conditions. Instead, it seems that Van Orden is correct in suggesting that the pronunciation of the presented word is generated and the categorization of the item is attempted in its phonological state. The effect of spelling similarity arises at a subsequent orthographic verification stage which is precluded when the stimulus is masked. There is no reason to suppose, however, that the pronunciation of the presented word is generated prior to lexical access. Instead, the pronunciation of the word could be found within its lexical entry, having been accessed on the basis of purely visual information.

Further work by Van Orden et al. (1988) addressed this point and concluded that the pronunciation was generated pre-access rather than post-access. The basis for this conclusion was that as many false positives were made in the semantic classification task with nonwords as with words. For example, as many errors were made in saying that JEAP was A VEHICLE as in saying that STEAL was A METAL. According to Van Orden et al. the errors made on nonwords could not have arisen from lexical information and, therefore, a pre-lexical mechanism is indicated. It does not necessarily follow, however, that the effect for word items arose from a pre-access stage just because the effect for words was of the same magnitude as that for nonwords. The semantic classification task presumably involves working memory which uses phonological representations (e.g. Baddeley, Eldridge, & Lewis, 1981; Kleiman, 1975), and it is in working memory where the false positive errors arise. Whether the phonological representation that enters working memory was generated pre- or post-access is not relevant. It may be the case that the phonological representation is generated by rule for nonwords, but determined from lexical information for words. What is needed to ascertain whether this is true or not is an experiment using the same paradigm with irregular words. If false positive errors are demonstrated in responding, for example, to SUITE as A FLAVOUR, then a post-lexical explanation is required, since the pronunciation of SUITE cannot be determined by pre-lexical rules.

Using yet another paradigm, Humphreys, Evett, & Taylor (1982) provide support for the post-access account of the involvement of phonology in reading. They employed a priming paradigm whereby the prime word was masked by the target word and the target word was masked by a pattern of letter fragments. Subjects were simply required to identify the masked target word. What Humphreys et al. found was that a word was more often correctly identified when preceded by a word which was homophonic with it than when preceded by a word which was only visually similar. For example, subjects identified STAIR more often when it was preceded by STARE than when it was preceded by STARK. While this result could be explained in terms of pre-lexical GPC rule application or GGC rule application, a further result suggested a post-lexical explanation. In particular, the same priming effect did not occur when the prime was a homophonic nonword. For example, identification of BRAIN was the same whether it was preceded by BRANE or BRANT. So it seems that the pronunciation of the prime that facilitates the identifiability of the homophonic target word is determined from lexical information. Since a nonword has no lexical entry, its pronunciation does not become available in the masked priming paradigm.

On the other hand, Perfetti, Bell, & Delaney (1988) come out in favour of pre-lexical phonological processing using a backward masking paradigm. A word was briefly presented, masked by a following nonword which, in turn, was masked by a row of X's. The subject's task was to identify the word. As opposed to the forward masking paradigm of Humphreys et al. (1982) this backward masking technique produced facilitation arising from homophony of the nonword with the word. For example, subjects identified BRAIN more often when it was followed by BRANE than when it was followed by BRANT. Putting aside the ever-present criticism that this result could be explained in terms of rule-governed orthographic similarity, it is difficult to reconcile the results of Perfetti et al. with those of Humphreys et al. and as such it is difficult to draw conclusions about lexical processing using a masked word identification task. It is doubtful, in fact, whether the task taps on-line processing anyway, especially in the case of the Perfetti et al. study where the response to the target word was influenced by information following that word.

Conclusions Regarding Homophony

It seems then that research on homophony and pseudohomophony is restricted in what it can say about phonological recoding in reading. Either the findings can be accounted for by supposing that they arise from orthographic similarity rather than phonological identity, or the locus of the phonological effect cannot be specified. Rather than being used as a means of accessing a lexical entry, the pronunciation of a word might be determined only after its lexical entry has been accessed. The strongest evidence in favour of pre-lexical phonological recoding discussed so far is the finding of Treiman et al. that irregular words (like ARE) are often regularized when spoken in the "regular" sentence framework, while regular words (like AIR) are not "exceptionalized" when spoken in the "irregular" sentence framework. This result, however, is more an effect of regularity than homophony, and further, it entails that the word be overtly pronounced, which may bring into play mechanisms that are not typically involved in silent reading.

The effects of regularity will be discussed more fully later in this chapter, particularly in relation to overt pronunciation. But first, an outline will be given of other experimental paradigms which purport to demonstrate a phonological involvement in silent reading.

FORM-PRIMING

Meyer, Schvaneveldt, and Ruddy

Meyer et al. (1974) used the form-priming paradigm described in Chapter 2, whereby a word is presented for lexical decision preceded by another word which shares all letters but the first. For example, the stimulus word TRIBE might be preceded by the word BRIBE. What Meyer et al. did was manipulate the phonological relationship between the two words such that they either did or did not rhyme. For example, while BRIBE and TRIBE rhyme, COUCH and TOUCH do not. It was found that lexical decision responses to the target word were faster when preceded by a rhyming word (e.g. TRIBE preceded by BRIBE) compared to an unrelated word (e.g. TRIBE preceded by COUCH), but, more interestingly, responses were delayed when the target was preceded by a word with conflicting pronunciation (e.g. TOUCH preceded by COUCH) compared to an unrelated word (e.g. TOUCH preceded by BRIBE).

The interpretation that Meyer et al. give for this finding is that after prelexical grapheme-to-phoneme conversion has occurred, presentation of the same set of graphemes will bias the encoding mechanism to use the same set of conversion rules. If this process leads to a phonological representation of the second word that cannot be located in the phonological access system, this will delay the recognition of that word. So, the rules used to generate the pronunciation of COUCH will be attempted for TOUCH, but this will not produce a valid phonological representation. Therefore, Meyer et al. support the existence of pre-lexical phonological recoding in silent reading.

Other Interpretations

The encoding bias account that Meyer et al. give for their data has been shown to be wrong. Hillinger (1980) demonstrated the same pattern of priming when the prime and the target were both presented visually as when the prime was presented aurally and the target presented visually. Since an aural presentation does not involve grapheme-to-phoneme conversion there can be no encoding bias in the processing of the visual target word. Further, Hillinger demonstrated facilitation in lexical decision responses when the prime and target rhymed even though they were not orthographically similar. For example, MOON was primed by PRUNE to the same extent that it was primed by SPOON. Clearly this result could not have arisen from a repetition of the same grapheme-to-phoneme conversion procedure since MOON and PRUNE would require different conversion rules.

Although opposing the encoding bias explanation for priming effects, Hillinger still supports a pre-lexical recoding view. He suggests that the representation of a word in the phonological input system is activated when that word is presented visually and recoded into a phonological representation. This activation then spreads to other words which rhyme and which are therefore assumed to be closely linked to each other in the phonological input store. When one of these rhyming words is now visually presented, it will be converted into a phonological form and gain access to the already activated entry in the phonological input system.

This explanation is supported by the fact that no form-priming was observed when the prime was a nonword, which would have no entry in the phonological input store (e.g. FLOON did not facilitate the recognition of MOON). What Hillinger did not test, however, was the effect of priming with a pseudohomophone (e.g. PROON followed by MOON). According to Hillinger's explanation of priming, the pseudohomophone should access an entry in the phonological input system and therefore produce facilitation.

This prediction was tested in the author's laboratory on 30 subjects and found to be wanting. Using 24 target words, each appearing with a rhyming nonword prime (e.g. FLOON MOON), a rhyming pseudo-homophone prime (e.g. PROON MOON), and a nonrhyming nonword prime (e.g. SLITH MOON), no significant difference in lexical decision times was found between any of the conditions (mean reaction times of 741msec, 755msec, and 743msec respectively). Lexical decision times to the word targets which were preceded by word primes did show rhyming facilitation, although it should be added that the effect was stronger when the two words were visually similar than when they were not (mean reaction times were 692msec for SPOON MOON items, 724msec for PRUNE MOON items, and 762msec for BENCH MOON items). These results, then, fail to support the pre-lexical recoding position of Hillinger.

The inhibition effect observed by Meyer et al. on nonrhyming word pairs like COUCH TOUCH can be explained by Hillinger in terms of the conflict set up between the increase in activation of the target word in the orthographic input system (resulting from the orthographic similarity between the two words), and the lack of increase in activation of the target word in the phonological input system. Shulman, Hornak, and Sanders (1978) found that nonrhyming pairs were treated just like rhyming pairs (e.g. BRIBE TRIBE) when the nonwords used in the lexical decision experiment were illegal letter strings like FKLNI, that is, such pairs produced facilitation. This result was taken by Hillinger to mean that the phonological route to the lexicon is not used when discrimination between words and nonwords is made easy, and thus there can be no conflict between the visual route and the phonological route in these circumstances.

There is, however, a post-lexical account for these results which Shulman et al. favour. They propose that words are given a phonological representation, not in order to gain access to the lexicon, but in order to hold the words in working memory while further processing is undertaken at the post-access decision stage (the same conclusion drawn from studies on homophony using the acceptability paradigm). When the words are easily discriminated from the nonwords this extra processing is unnecessary and thus phonological representations are never required. The only facilitation in these circumstances would arise from the spreading of activation between orthographically similar lexical entries (i.e. both between BRIBE and TRIBE and between TOUCH and COUCH). When the words and nonwords are hard to discriminate, a strategy is adopted which makes use of the pronunciation of the letter strings. If the target word does not rhyme with the prime word, one is biased towards thinking that the wrong entry has been accessed, and therefore responses are delayed.

This post-access account could explain why FLOON does not prime MOON, by making the assumption that the phonological representation used in working memory is extracted from lexical information, and FLOON is not found in the lexicon. Furthermore, this position would predict that PROON would not facilitate the recognition of MOON, since PROON is not found in the lexicon either, and thus is consistent with my own results reported above. We can conclude, therefore, that the form-priming data are more consistent with a post-lexical than a pre-lexical determination of pronunciation during reading.

Is it the case though, that the reason why the pronunciation of a word is determined after the lexical entry has been accessed is solely for strategic purposes in performing a particular experimental task? One body of research suggests not. Instead, it is supposed that phonological recoding during silent reading is important when demands are placed upon working memory. This will now be briefly discussed.

ARTICULATORY SUPPRESSION

The assumption has been made that any phonological processing that occurs during silent reading will be suppressed if the reader is concurrently occupying the phonological system by articulating irrelevant material (e.g. Kleiman, 1975; Levy, 1977; M.Martin, 1978). Studies have therefore tried to determine if performance on a particular set of materials is disrupted by the concurrent articulation of irrelevant material, which would imply that phonological factors are involved in that task.

Kleiman (1975) was able to demonstrate that a task that required subjects to decide whether or not there was a word in a visually presented sentence which rhymed with a predesignated word (e.g. CREAM with DREAM, but not BURY with JURY) was more greatly affected by articulatory suppression than a task that required subjects to decide whether or not there was a word which graphemically "rhymed" with a predesignated word (e.g. BURY with JURY, but not GATHER with MOTHER). Such a result is not surprising since the former task explicitly involves the pronunciation of the word, whereas the latter explicitly does not. What was of greater interest was what happened in tasks directed at the meaning of the words.

In fact, there was very little effect of concurrent articulation on a task where subjects had to decide whether or not a sentence contained a member of a predesignated category (e.g. MONOPOLY is a GAME, but CARPENTRY is not a SPORT). However, there was a very large effect when the task was to decide whether or not a sentence was meaningful (e.g. NOISY PARTIES DISTURB SLEEPING NEIGHBOURS, but not PIZZAS HAVE BEEN EATING JERRY). This pattern of results suggests that a phonological version of the words of a sentence is required when that sentence, or part of that sentence, needs to be held in working memory so that processing can be carried out upon it. Such would be the case when attempting to comprehend a reasonably difficult sentence.

Kleiman's study therefore provides a reason for phonological recoding to occur other than for purposes of access to the lexicon via the phonological input system. Studies by Besner, Davies, and Daniels (1981) and Besner and Davelaar (1982) provide evidence for the existence of both types of phonological code; one for maintaining information in working memory and one for gaining access to lexical information.

In one of Besner and Davelaar's experiments, for example, subjects were visually presented with a list of four items that were to be orally recalled either with or without concurrent articulation. Lists were either phonologically confusable in that the four items rhymed with each other, or they were not. In addition, half of the items were pseudohomophones (e.g. NEWD) and half were not (e.g. ZEWD). Nonconfusable items were better recalled than confusable items and pseudohomophones were better recalled than nonhomophonic nonwords, but what was of central interest was that the confusability effect was eliminated by articulatory suppression while the homophony effect was unaffected by it (although the overall recall performance was much diminished by articulatory suppression). It was concluded from these data that the confusability effect reflects phonological confusions within working memory. Since concurrent articulation prevents a phonological representation from being set up in working memory, recall performance is poor and is unmodulated by confusability. The phonological code that is involved in the homophony effect, on the other hand, is seen as a code that is used to gain access to lexical information. Articulatory suppression leaves this code untouched, presumably because it is developed at a level that is more abstract than articulation.

Research into articulatory suppression, however, has more to say about the reason for generating a phonological code during silent reading, rather than the mechanisms involved in so doing. We turn now to the approach which has probably been the most productive in what it suggests about phonological processes in visual lexical access.

REGULARITY EFFECTS

Defining Regularity

In addition to homophony, rhyme, and concurrent articulation, a variable that can be manipulated in an attempt to tap phonological processing in visual word recognition is grapheme-to-phoneme regularity. A grapheme will be defined here as any letter or group of letters that stands for a single phoneme or diphthong (or in the case of X, a single letter that stands for more than one phoneme). A regular grapheme-phoneme relationship is one where the phoneme is the most typical pronunciation of the grapheme. For example, the grapheme OO is regularly pronounced as /u:/, and the grapheme EA has the regular pronunciation /i:/. Therefore, SPOOK, SPOON, TREAT, and STEAL are all regular words, while CROOK, BLOOD, SWEAT, and BREAK are all irregular or exception words.

As was pointed out earlier, the mere fact that we can comprehend irregular words is evidence that reading does not entail phonological recoding. For example, the word CROOK, recoded by rule as /kru:k/ (i.e. rhyming with SPOOK), would not be found in the phonological input store, while the word SWEAT would always be translated as /swi:t/ and confused with SWEET or SUITE. One could perhaps counter this argument by saying that the phonological input store actually contains the representation /kru:k/ for the purposes of recognizing CROOK. However, this would mean that the actual utterance /kru:k/ should be immediately and unquestionably recognized as CROOK, and this is obviously not the case.

Information about the correct pronunciation of an irregular word can only be determined from information stored within its lexical entry, and therefore, only a direct visual route to the lexicon can be used in recognizing irregular words. The question then becomes whether there actually does exist an additional indirect phonological route to the lexicon, as the dual-route model suggests (e.g. M.Coltheart, 1978, 1980). One way of addressing this question has been to compare performance on irregular words and regular words.

Predictions from the Dual-route Model

According to the dual-route model, lexical access is attempted via both a direct visual pathway and an indirect phonological pathway, with the two routes being used in parallel. If this is correct, it is reasonable to suppose that conflicting outcomes from the two routes will retard recognition. The potential for conflicting outcomes is provided by irregular words. The strongest form of conflict would arise in the recognition of a word like SWEAT which would access a different word via the phonological route (i.e. SWEET or SUITE) than it would via the visual route (SWEAT). A weaker form of conflict arises with the more common type of irregular word, like CROOK or BLOOD, where the visual route would be successful while the phonological route would suggest that there is no appropriate lexical entry and that the letter string is therefore not a word.

There have been no reported studies of the strongly conflicting words in a lexical decision task, but there have been several examinations of the weaker conflicting words. These studies (e.g. Andrews, 1982; M. Coltheart, Besner, Jonasson, & Davelaar, 1979; Mason, 1978; Seidenberg, Waters, Barnes, & Tanenhaus, 1984b) have typically found that irregular words are not associated with longer lexical decision times than regular words.[2] However, this is perhaps not surprising even according to the dual-route model.

While there is the potential for conflict in the case of irregular words, the standard dual-route model proposes that the visual pathway is faster than the phonological pathway. The phonological pathway will only come into play when the visual route is slow or unsuccessful. Thus phonological effects will only be observed with low frequency words or nonwords. This does not mean, though, that regularity effects should necessarily be observed in lexical decision times to low frequency words. Although the visual route will be slower for low frequency words than for high frequency words, when the word is irregular the representation entering the phonological route will be a nonword. Therefore, the phonological route will still take longer to reach an outcome than the visual route, so there is no reason for conflict to occur. The best test of conflict between the two routes would be to examine lexical decision times to words like SWEAT where the phonological route would quickly access the inappropriate high frequency word /swi:t/ (i.e. SWEET), but no one has reported such a study (as also pointed out by Henderson, 1985a).

Another way of getting the phonological route to reach an outcome at approximately the same time as the visual route is to require subjects to actually produce a pronunciation. When the word to be pronounced is a low frequency word, access to the lexically stored pronunciation might take long enough for the nonlexically generated pronunciation to emerge at about the same time. If so, the time taken to initiate a naming response to a low frequency exception word should be longer than that to a low frequency regular word, since the two pronunciations would be in conflict in the former case, but not in the latter case.

The finding of longer naming responses to irregular words compared to regular words was observed by Baron and Strawson (1976) and Stanovich and Bauer (1978) amongst others, with Andrews (1982) and Seidenberg et al. (1984b) indicating that such an effect is only evident for low frequency words. Such a finding is therefore consistent with the dual-route model. However, the latter two authors come out in favour of a single-route model, inspired by an influential study carried out by Glushko (1979).

THE CONSISTENCY EFFECT

Glushko (1979) demonstrated an effect which would not be predicted by the standard dual-route model. The regular word TREAT and the irregular word THREAT have the same final multi-letter pattern (called a "body" by Patterson & Morton, 1985). The body-EAT can be said to have an "inconsistent" pronunciation in that it is not always pronounced in the same way, unlike the consistent body-EAN, which is invariably pronounced as /i:n/. What Glushko found was that words like TREAT which are regular but inconsistent, took longer to name than words like CLEAN which are regular and consistent. According to the dual-route model, all regular words will be given their correct pronunciation via the rule-mediated phonological route regardless of the consistency of their body, and therefore should not be in conflict with the pronunciation extracted from the visually accessed lexical entry. So the finding of a delay caused by inconsistency is a major problem for the dual-route model.

Further studies have replicated the consistency effect with a number of refinements being made. For example, Seidenberg et al. (1984b) demonstrated that the effect only held for low frequency words and, along with Stanhope and Parkin (1987), showed that it was inflated by the prior presentation in the word list of the irregular version of the word body. Andrews (1982) found that irregular words were also affected by consistency, such that an irregular word whose body was always pronounced in the same way, like MALT (cf. HALT and SALT), was associated with faster naming times than an inconsistent irregular word, like CROW (cf. BROW). The influence on the effect of the number of words with conflicting pronunciations was demonstrated by Kay and Bishop (1987) who found that there was a delay in naming either a regular or an exception word only when the pronunciation of its body was the least common pronunciation for that body. For example, the body-ILD is more commonly pronounced /aɪld/ than /ɪld/ and therefore there would be a delay in naming the regular word GILD, but not in naming the irregular word MILD. Conversely, there are more words in which-INT is pronounced /ɪnt/ than /aɪnt/ and therefore there would be a delay in naming the irregular word PINT, but no delay in naming the regular word HINT. A similar result was obtained by Parkin (1984).

A Single-route Model

Even with these refinements, Glushko's account of the consistency effect still has currency. He puts forward the view that pronunciations are always derived from lexical information, and never by rule. This is achieved via an activation-synthesis mechanism, which McClelland and Rumelhart (1981) have incorporated into their interactive-activation model. Word bodies form a set of units that are intermediate between letter cluster units (like SPL and ND) and word units. When a unit becomes activated on the basis of orthographic input, associated phonological units become activated as well. So when CLEAN is presented, the orthographic units CL, EA, EAN, and CLEAN (amongst others) become activated, which in turn will activate /kl/, /iː/, /iːn/ and /kliːn/. The correct pronunciation is then synthesized from this phonological information. When TREAT is presented, however, there is conflicting phonological information since the unit EAT will activate both /iːt/ (as in TREAT) and /ɛt/ (as in THREAT), not to mention /eɪt/ (as in GREAT).

If it is further assumed that the frequency of the association between a graphemic unit and a phonemic unit influences the amount of activation in the phonemic unit, it is easy to explain why there is more conflict in synthesizing the correct pronunciation when the word body has a rarely occurring pronunciation than when it has a common one (Kay & Bishop, 1987). Similarly, it follows that the weaker the activation of the whole word pronunciation (i.e. the lower the frequency of the word), the greater the influence of conflicting body pronunciations and therefore, the consistency effect should be greater for low frequency words than high frequency words (Seidenberg et al., 1984b). Finally, since nonwords (like TREAN) can be pronounced in the same way that words are, namely, by synthesizing a pronunciation from activated phonological knowledge, only the lexical route is required for pronouncing all letter strings.

While this type of single-route notion is able to explain the consistency effect (and is indeed designed to do so), and despite receiving considerable acceptance elsewhere (e.g. Andrews, 1982; Humphreys & Evett, 1985; Seidenberg et al., 1984b), it suffers a number of potential problems. First, there is an issue raised by Seidenberg et al. but not answered by them, and that is the question of how the final correct pronunciation is settled upon. The correct pronunciation must ultimately be based on the phonological representation associated with the whole word unit, at least in the case of inconsistent words. Yet if the pronunciation can be determined from whole word units, why is the system designed to synthesize a pronunciation from subword units, particularly given that this will often lead to conflict? A possible solution to this will be offered later in this chapter, where a version of the interactive-activation model is described which contains no whole word phonological units.

Neuropsychological Evidence

There is another potential problem facing the single-route account of the derivation of pronunciation from print, which arises from neuropsychological research. The study of acquired dyslexia has provided data that has been taken to be inconsistent with a single-route view (e.g. M. Coltheart, 1985). Acquired dyslexia involves a dysfunction in lexical access mechanisms arising from lesions within a previously normally functioning adult brain (e.g. as a result of a stroke or an accident) and one can identify a variety of symptom complexes (see M. Coltheart et al., 1980; Patterson et al., 1985).

In one type of dyslexia ("surface dyslexia", e.g. Bub, Cancelliere, & Kertesz, 1985), the symptoms that are observed include an inability to comprehend and correctly pronounce irregular words, while performance on regular words and on nonwords is intact. Furthermore, the pronunciations that are given to irregular words tend to be regularizations (e.g. /pɪnt/ for PINT). These symptoms are exactly those that would be expected if a direct visual route to the lexicon were disrupted while an indirect phonological route were intact. Letter strings could only be named via pronunciation rules, and therefore, irregular pronunciations would be precluded.[3]

What is even more impressive is that one can find a second type of acquired dyslexia ("phonological dyslexia", e.g. Funnell, 1983) which reflects exactly what one would expect if it were the phonological route rather than the visual route that was disrupted. According to the dual-route position, lexical information which is accessed via the visual route provides the pronunciation for all words, be they regular or irregular, but not for nonwords which can only be pronounced via nonlexical rule application. Therefore, if the lexical route to pronunciation is intact, but the nonlexical route is disrupted, performance on naming nonwords should be very poor while both regular and irregular words should be comprehended and pronounced quite readily. This is exactly the pattern observed in phonological dyslexia.

For the single-route model to explain this double dissociation between symptom complexes, it must be assumed that whole word units and sublexical units can be differentially disrupted (Humphreys & Evett, 1985). The pattern of performance observed in surface dyslexia can be explained if the links between the whole word units and their phonological representations are lost while the sublexical units remain intact. In this case pronunciations can only be assembled from sublexical units and this will produce appropriate pronunciations for regular words and nonwords, but regularizations for exception words. If the converse occurs, namely, if the links between word units and their phonological representations are intact while those between sublexical units and their phonological representations are lost, the phonological dyslexic pattern of performance will emerge. All words will be able to be pronounced, while nonwords will not.

The Dual-route and Single-route Models Converge

Once one allows for a dissociation between word units and sublexical units, however, this model becomes essentially equivalent to a dual-route account. That is, it says that pronunciations can be derived in two different ways; pronunciations can be assembled from the phonological representations associated with sublexical units (i.e. a nonlexical route) or they can be determined from the phonological representation associated with the whole word (i.e. a lexical route). What is different between this account and the traditional dual-route model is that the nonlexical route now takes into account units larger than the single grapheme. Such a position has been adopted by Shallice, Warrington, and McCarthy (1983) and Shallice and McCarthy (1985), who propose that phonological recoding is based on graphemic units ranging in size from single graphemes to morphemes, while Patterson and Morton (1985) include both single graphemes and word bodies in their nonlexical phonological route. As pointed out by G.D. Brown (1987), and Patterson and V. Coltheart (1987), once one introduces multiple levels of translation from spelling to sound, the distinction between dual-route and single-route models becomes extremely blurred.

A MULTIPLE-LEVELS MODEL

What I will now present is a multiple-levels model which is derived from the interactive-activation account. The model is intended to illustrate how some of the results which have been hard for single-level models to accommodate can be explained.

It can be seen from the version of the interactive-activation model depicted in Fig. 4.1 that activation can occur in orthographically defined units at the grapheme, letter cluster, and word body levels, and in phonologically defined units at the phoneme, phoneme cluster, and word body levels. One interesting aspect of the model is that there is no level of orthographic representation nor phonological representation for the whole word. Instead, information about the whole word is represented at a level of "concept" nodes which mediates between lexical memory and semantic memory. By using the label "concept nodes", I do not wish to imply that the meaning of a word is represented in a single node; it is merely shorthand to describe nodes which, when activated, provide a pathway to the meaning of the word. The reason for adopting this approach is simply that a representation of the orthography and phonology of the whole word is redundant, in that all the necessary information about the orthography and phonology of the whole word can be found in the combination of clusters and bodies.

Activation begins at the lowest level of unit (i.e. the graphemic level when the stimuli are visually presented, and the phonemic level when the stimuli are spoken)[4], and passes up to the higher level units via the appropriate connections (depicted as unbroken lines in Fig. 4.1). Activation passes back down from the higher units to the lower units, and in the case of the concept units, such activation passes down to both orthographic and phonological units even though the stimulus was presented in only one modality. The broken lines in Fig. 4.1 represent connections which directly link the orthographic and phonological units. These connections have their most important role when the task specifically requires a phonological response to a visual stimulus, like naming and homophone decision (or an orthographic response to a spoken stimulus, like spelling to dictation).

It should be noted, however, that it would be quite possible to dispense with the cluster level of units since they provide little more than that contained in the grapheme and phoneme units. The cluster level was simply included because research by Treiman and colleagues (e.g. Treiman & Chafetz, 1987; Treiman, Goswami, & Bruck, 1990; Treiman & Zukowski, 1988) has shown that monosyllabic words appear to be treated as being made up of an initial cluster and a body (or "onset" and "rime").

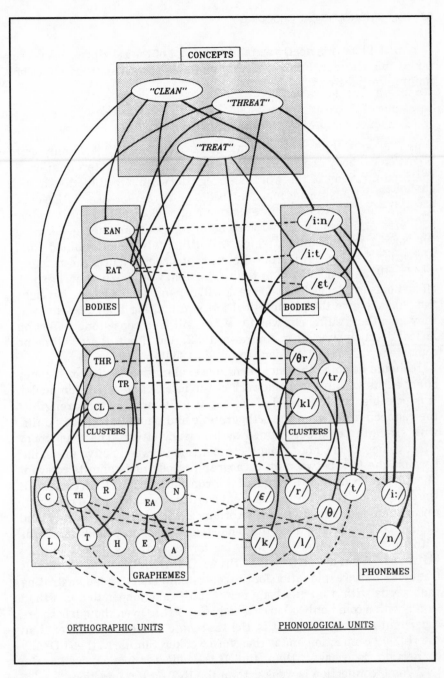

FIG. 4.1 A subset of a version of the interactive–activation model incorporating body units

A model like this neatly accounts for most of the results discussed so far in this chapter. First, it clearly explains the consistency effect on naming responses.

Explaining the Consistency Effect

When a word has a consistent body, as does CLEAN, only one phonological body node is activated and therefore the determination of the pronunciation of the word is straightforward. On the other hand, when a word has an inconsistent body, be it regular (e.g. TREAT) or irregular (e.g. THREAT), more than one phonological body unit will be activated and these will therefore be in competition when generating the correct pronunciation, which will ultimately be determined from activation feeding down from the concept nodes. Hence, inconsistent words will take longer to name than consistent words. Whether the same effect holds in a lexical decision task will depend upon how much weight the subjects give the phonological units in making their responses. If they give them sufficient weight, there will be a consistency effect on lexical decision times (e.g. Andrews, 1982), but if not, there will be no consistency effect (e.g. Seidenberg et al., 1984b).

It should be noted that an alternative explanation for the consistency effect exists within the framework of the interactive-activation model. It is possible that the speed of naming is influenced by the strength of the connection between the orthographic and phonological body units, with strength being determined by frequency of use. The consistency effect comes about, not through competition between active units, but because the link between an orthographic body node and its relevant phonological body node is weaker for inconsistent words than consistent words, although only for inconsistent words whose body has a relatively uncommon pronunciation. In accordance with this idea is Kay and Bishop's (1987) finding that the consistency effect only holds for words with the least common pronunciation for its body (e.g. GILD, but not MILD; PINT, but not MINT). G.D. Brown (1987) indirectly supports this frequency based explanation for the consistency effect by demonstrating that words with a unique body (e.g. FILM) take longer to name than words with a commonly occurring body (e.g. FILL) even though both are consistent and regular. That is, the ILM–/ɪlm/ connection is rarer than the ILL–/ɪl/ connection and is therefore weaker. Similarly, the ILD–/ɪld/ connection is weaker than the ILD–/aɪld/ connection, while the INT–/aɪnt/ connection is weaker than the INT–/ɪnt/ connection.

However, just because the relatively slow responses to words with unique bodies (like FILM) can be interpreted in terms of frequency, it does not mean that, at the same time, the relatively slow responses to inconsistent words (like PINT) cannot be interpreted in terms of competition. It may be the case that frequency has its effects by influencing the amount of activation within the phonological and/or orthographic nodes (i.e. their resting level of activation), rather than the strength of the link between them. If so, the consistency effect could come about because of competition between a weakly active node (e.g. /aɪnt/) and a more strongly active node (e.g. /ɪnt/), while the relatively slow responses to FILM compared to FILL would come about because the node for /ɪlm/ has a lower resting level of activation than has the node for /ɪl/.

Whether the consistency effect is best explained in terms of competition between units or in terms of frequency of activation (see Seidenberg & McClelland, 1989, for arguments favouring the competition explanation), it does not alter the basic framework as depicted in Fig. 4.1.

Explaining Neighbourhood Effects

In Chapter 2, we saw that experiments manipulating neighbourhood size (i.e. the number of words which are one letter different from the stimulus word) demonstrated that the larger the neighbourhood, the faster the response times to a word, both for naming and for lexical decision (e.g. Andrews, 1989). The explanation for this was given in terms of the supportive activation from the nodes representing the neighbouring words (Andrews, 1989). Yet, if one incorporates the notion of inhibition into the interactive-activation model (as does McClelland and Rumelhart, 1981), such a view is unsatisfactory in that there is as likely to be inhibition arising from the nodes representing the neighbouring words as there is facilitation. There is an alternative explanation for the neighbourhood size effect, however, which is still within the framework of the interactive-activation model.

Most of the words in the neighbourhood of a stimulus word are likely to be words which differ from the stimulus word on their first letter (e.g. HAND, LAND, BAND, SAND, etc.). Because of this, neighbourhood size is very likely to be confounded with frequency of body and, therefore, the neighbourhood size effect can be seen as being equivalent to G.D. Brown's result where response times were influenced by the frequency of the body of the stimulus word. In this way, the neighbourhood size effect is no longer seen as being an effect of facilitation, but rather can be seen as being an effect of either the resting levels of activation of the body units or the strength of the connections between the orthographic and phonological body units.

A recent result obtained the author's laboratory is consistent with this position. Pairs of words which were matched on neighbourhood density, but varied on body frequency were compared. It was found that lexical decision times to words like WHEEL (a word with no neighbours, but whose body EEL is common, e.g. in FEEL, HEEL, STEEL, REEL, KNEEL, EEL, etc.) were significantly shorter than those to words like CLAIM (also a word with no neighbours, but whose body AIM is rare — occurring only in CLAIM, MAIM, and AIM). What still needs to be examined though are words matched on body frequency, but varying on neighbourhood density in order to establish that they do not differ. For example, CLAIM could be compared to SAFE, which also shares its body with only two other words (i.e. CHAFE and CAFE), but differs from several other words by one letter (e.g. SAVE, SALE, SAME, CAFE).

Explaining the Neuropsychological Evidence

A model of reading needs to explain how some acquired dyslexics are far worse at reading nonwords than both regular and irregular words (phonological dyslexia) while other dyslexics are far worse at reading irregular words than regular words and nonwords (surface dyslexia). As was pointed out earlier, the interactive-activation model needs to allow for a differential disruption of the whole word unit system and the sublexical unit system.

In terms of the model as depicted in Fig. 4.1, phonological dyslexia would come about through the disruption of the direct links between the orthographic units and the phonological units (i.e. the broken lines). Without these links, one would still be able to pronounce any word via activation in the phonological units that has come down from the "whole word" concept units. Nonwords would be unable to be pronounced because there are no concept nodes for nonwords, and therefore there would be minimal activation being passed to the phonological units.

Surface dyslexia would be explained in terms of a disruption to the links connecting the concept nodes to the orthographic units. The only pathway to pronunciation would be via the direct links between the orthographic and phonological units and, therefore, the only basis for deciding which pronunciation to give to a particular body would be the frequency of that pronunciation. Because of this, an irregular pronunciation would rarely be given.

Note that a disruption to the connection between concept units and phonological units would lead to the same symptoms as the proposed disruption to the connection between concept units and orthographic units. The reason why the latter is the preferred account has to do with the fact that when surface dyslexics report the meaning of a word, they appear to base it on the word that they pronounced, even though that pronunciation might be incorrect (e.g. M.Coltheart, Masterson, Byng,

Prior, & Riddoch, 1983). For example, a surface dyslexic might say that the word SWEAT means "sugary" because they have pronounced it as /swi:t/ through the connection between the body units EAT and /i:t/, and then activated the concept unit for "sweet" via this pronunciation. If it were the connections to the phonological units that were disrupted rather than those to the orthographic units, the meaning that was generated would be based on the orthographic version of the word rather than the phonological version.

An Alternative to Grapheme-to-Grapheme Rules

In addition to clarifying the interactive-activation explanation for consistency effects and the different dyslexic symptom complexes, the model illustrated in Fig. 4.1 provides an account of other troublesome findings that have been described in this chapter. In particular, the model offers an alternative explanation for the results that were previously taken as support for the unappealing notion of grapheme-to-grapheme conversion rules (Taft, 1982).

First, the fact that the similarity of DEEF to DEAF causes as much of a delay to lexical decision responses as does the similarity of LEEF to LEAF, can be explained in the following way (see Van Orden et al., 1988). When LEEF is presented, the concept node for LEAF is activated via the pathways passing from the grapheme node EE to the phoneme node /i:/, from the phoneme node /i:/ to the phonological body node /i:f/, and from the phonological body node /i:f/ to the orthographic body node EAF. The concept node for DEAF is activated via exactly the same route when DEEF is presented, and therefore, there is as much interference to response times for DEEF as for LEEF.

Secondly, the delay in lexical decision responses to items like CHALC, compared to items like HALC, arises when the concept node for CHALK is activated. The grapheme node representing the final C activates the phoneme node /k/ which in turn activates the grapheme node K, and the orthographic body node ALK is then activated by the grapheme nodes A, L, and K, which in turn activates the concept node for CHALK. On the other hand, the concept node for HAWK is not directly activated through the body node ALK, which is activated when HALC is presented. It should be noted, however, that access to the concept node for HAWK is possible via the ALK–/ɔ:k/ link and therefore, there should be some interference to the response to HALC. However, the response to CHALC also accrues interference via the ALK–/ɔ:k/ link and this is additional to the interference generated by the activation passing directly from the ALK node to the CHALK node.

In addition, it is easier to say that SKREAM is homophonic with a word than is SKREME, as the concept node for SCREAM is directly activated by the orthographic body node EAM (as well as the phonological body node /iːm/), but not by the orthographic body node EME.

It can therefore be seen that all the results that were taken as support for the existence of grapheme-to-grapheme rules can alternatively be explained in terms of interactive-activation.

Explaining Form-priming

The interactive-activation model runs into some difficulty when attempting to explain the finding of priming on the basis of rhyme (e.g. SPOON MOON and PRUNE MOON versus BENCH MOON). The explanation put forward earlier in the chapter was a post-access strategy. If the pronunciation extracted from the lexical entry of the prime and the target coincide in some way (i.e. if they rhyme), then there is a bias toward saying that the target is a word. When the pronunciation cannot be extracted from the lexicon there is no such bias (as in FLOON MOON and PROON MOON) and therefore no priming is observed (i.e. compared to SLITH MOON). The interactive-activation model offers a different explanation.

Priming comes about through the vestige of activation remaining within a previously activated unit (i.e. an increase in resting level). For example, the OON unit is activated when SPOON is presented and is still partly activated when MOON is presented and hence, the criterion level of activation is reached more quickly than if MOON were preceded by BENCH. Similarly, the /uːn/ unit is activated by the prior presentation of both SPOON and PRUNE and therefore there should be facilitation of responses to MOON when preceded by PRUNE, but more so when preceded by SPOON. This is the pattern of results obtained in my unpublished study (see earlier), though not quite the pattern obtained in Hillinger's study, where PRUNE was as effective a prime as SPOON.

The potential difficulty for the interactive-activation account arises when we consider the nonword primes. Since facilitation is supposedly emanating from the vestigial activation in the orthographic and phonological body nodes, nonwords should be able to prime word targets. Yet they do not. For example, FLOON activates the unit OON and therefore the response to the target word MOON should benefit from this. In order to explain why it does not, the model must add in certain conditions. One possibility is to say that if no concept node reaches the acceptance threshold (i.e. if a nonword response is given), then the activation level in all sublexical units immediately returns to its normal resting state. Hence, there would be no vestigial activation when the target is presented.

If this is the correct explanation, it should be the case that while nonword primes do not affect responses to rhyming word targets, word primes should adversely influence responses to rhyming nonword targets (e.g. MOON FLOON versus SLOW FLOON). The decision that FLOON is not a word should be delayed by any activation in the OON and /uːn/ body units remaining from the prior presentation of MOON. The data which Hillinger (1980) report fail to demonstrate this interference on reaction times, but there does appear to be a strong effect on errors. Such an effect would not have been predicted by the post-access strategy account, since the post-access matching process was assumed to be carried out on pronunciations extracted from the lexicon, and therefore, having a nonword in either the prime or the target position should have eliminated any bias. Therefore, the interactive-activation account has the capacity to offer the most preferable explanation for the form-priming results, although at the expense of requiring an assumption that has yet to be independently motivated.

It should be noted, however, that quite a different pattern of form-priming is obtained when the prime is masked (e.g. Forster, 1987; Forster et al., 1987). Here, nonwords do facilitate lexical decision times to words (e.g. FLOON MOON) while nonword targets are not facilitated by a form-related prime (e.g. MOON FLOON). The former result is predicted by the interactive-activation account without the need for any additional assumptions, but now the latter result requires further consideration. Perhaps it can be said that the increased activation in the body node (that would facilitate response times to a word target) is counterbalanced by a delay in the nonword deadline arising from that increased activation.

We can see then, that the instantiation of the multiple-levels notion depicted in Fig. 4.1 is quite a fruitful way of thinking about lexical processing and the involvement of phonology in orthographic processing. There is one further challenge, however, which confronts any attempt at modelling phonological involvement in visual lexical processing. This is the method by which nonwords are given a pronunciation.

PRONOUNCING NONWORDS

Nonword Pronunciation Consistency

According to the multiple levels view, nonwords are pronounced by assembling a pronunciation from the phonological representations of the sublexical units. Another way of putting this is to say that nonwords are pronounced by analogy to real words. For example, the pronunciation of TREAN as /triːn/ comes about because EAN is pronounced /iːn/ in CLEAN, MEAN, BEAN, etc. and TR is pronounced /tr/ in TRUCK, TRAY, etc. This view, as opposed to the traditional single-level dual-route model, predicts that it will take longer to assemble a pronunciation when the nonword has an inconsistent body like SMEAD, than when it has a consistent body like TREAN, since in the former case there will be conflict in deciding which pronunciation to give (i.e. /smiːd/ or /smɛd/). Glushko (1979) has reported such a result. There is no reason for SMEAD to take longer to name than TREAN if pronunciation were based solely on grapheme-phoneme rules, as the traditional dual-route model supposes, since the consistency of units larger than EA should be irrelevant.

Pronunciation Priming

A further finding which has been taken as support for an analogy model of nonword naming is that the pronunciation of an inconsistent nonword can be biased by the pronunciation of a previously presented word (Kay & Marcel, 1981; Taraban & McClelland, 1987). For example, presentation of the word BEAD prior to SMEAD is more likely to lead to a /smiːd/ pronunciation than prior presentation of THREAD, which is more likely to lead to a /smɛd/ pronunciation. Such biasing in pronunciation seems to happen even when the prior word is only semantically related to a word with the same body as the nonword (Rosson, 1983). For example, prior presentation of NEEDLE, being semantically related to the word THREAD, increases the proportion of occasions that SMEAD is pronounced /smɛd/.

These priming results have been taken as strong support for the analogy model since, according to the model, pronunciations of nonwords are lexically influenced and therefore have the potential to be biased by existing lexical items. However, it is not impossible to explain these results in terms of the traditional single-level dual-route model. What one could suggest is that when there is ambiguity in grapheme-to-phoneme translation, this ambiguity is resolved by recourse to lexical information. Such is the theory put forward by P. Brown and Besner (1987).

An Alternative Single-level Model

According to this proposal, the grapheme EA would be associated with both an /iː/ translation and an /ɛ/ translation, and therefore both /smiːd/ and /smɛd/ would become candidate pronunciations. These pronunciations would then be fed into the lexicon via the phonological input system to determine which is more similar to an existing word, and choice of pronunciation would be based on the outcome of this decision. Prior presentation of THREAD or NEEDLE would activate the lexical entry for THREAD and hence the choice of pronunciation for SMEAD would be biased toward the THREAD-like pronunciation.

In fact, P. Brown and Besner offer this candidate selection view as an explanation for all oral reading, not just for nonword naming. In order to explain how irregular words like YACHT are pronounced, they would have to postulate the existence of nonproductive rules like CHT → /t/ and A→/ɒ/, so that the pronunciation /jɒt/ can be submitted to the phonological input system for recognition. In addition, there needs to be a post-lexical orthographic check in order that a decision can be made on how to pronounce a word like SWEAT for which there are two acceptable phonological conversions (i.e. /swi:t/ as well as /swɛt/).

The reason why P. Brown and Besner favour a model like this rather than an analogy model, is that they observed patterns of nonword naming which were inconsistent with the notion that nonwords are pronounced by analogy to real words having the same body. For example, the pronunciation given to a monosyllabic nonword ending in OUN seemed to be biased by whether the pronunciation /aʊn/ or /u:n/ led to a real word or not. So, FROUN tended to be pronounced /fraʊn/ as in FROWN, while relatively more /u:n/ pronunciations were given for JOUN, SOUN, TOUN, and DOUN, to make them homophonic with JUNE, SOON, and North American TUNE and DUNE. If these nonwords were being named via analogy to words with an OUN body, P. Brown and Besner claim that they should have all been given the same pronunciation, namely, /aʊn/ as in NOUN (the only word in English with the body OUN).

However, this claim is not really true. According to the interactive-activation model, activation of the grapheme node OU will activate both the /aʊ/ and /u:/ phoneme nodes which will feed activation up to the /aʊn/ and /u:n/ body nodes. If the nonword stimulus is FROUN, for example, the combined activation of the nodes /fr/ and /aʊn/ will activate the concept node for FROWN and this in turn will feed back down to the phonological units and strengthen the /aʊn/ node. In this way the /fraʊn/ pronunciation will triumph over the /fru:n/ pronunciation because of the existence of the former as a word. Thus, P. Brown and Besner's results are perfectly compatible with at least this version of the analogy model.

Nonwords with Consistent, Irregular Bodies

A problem facing P. Brown and Besner's candidate selection view, but one which is also a challenge to the analogy model, is the way in which nonwords like DACHT are pronounced. Here, the body is only ever pronounced irregularly in real English words (as in YACHT). According to P. Brown and Besner, DACHT should be recoded by rule into /dɒt/ (just as YACHT is recoded into /jɒt/) which will gain access to the lexical entry for DOT via the phonological input system. Therefore, DACHT should be pronounced /dɒt/, but such a pronunciation, I have found, is extremely rare. The analogy model also seems to predict a /dɒt/ pronunciation since the only word on which to base the analogy is YACHT.

In an unpublished study (Taft & Cottrell, 1988), subjects were presented with a number of nonwords whose body was consistently pronounced irregularly in real words (e.g. BALF as in HALF and CALF; ZOLK as in FOLK and YOLK; SNALD as in BALD and SCALD). It was found that the regular pronunciation was given significantly more often than the irregular (i.e. /bælf/ rather than /bɑːf/, /zolk/ rather than /zoʊk/, /snæld/ rather than /snɔːld/) and further, that when the irregular pronunciation was given, the response was significantly slower than the regular pronunciation. If analogy were the dominant method by which pronunciations are generated, then the irregular (consistent) pronunciations should have been favoured in these cases.

To explain these data in terms of an analogy type of model, one needs to suppose that the commonly occurring pronunciations of the units smaller than the body (e.g. OL–/ol/) override the less common body pronunciations (like OLK–/oʊk/). In terms of the interactive-activation model depicted in Fig. 4.1, one needs to say that when little activation is being passed down to the phonological body units from the concept units, as in the case of a nonword, the pronunciation tends to rely on the lower level phoneme units. Given that this assumption is *ad hoc*, however, there needs to be independent motivation for it before accepting that the interactive-activation model can account for nonword pronunciations.

OVERVIEW

The original controversy in relation to phonological processes in visual lexical access was whether an indirect phonological route to the lexicon is required in silent reading. The answer based on research into homophony, form-priming, and regularity seemed to be negative and instead a dual-route model was proposed. By this account, normal silent reading takes place via direct visual access with phonological representations extracted from the lexicon for use in working memory. The indirect phonological route is seen as a back-up route which only comes into play when access via the direct visual route proves difficult or impossible. However, the phonological nature of this back-up mechanism in silent reading was questioned by the possibility that it might actually be orthographic in nature.

Increasingly, controversy in this area has centred upon the question of whether or not the indirect phonological pathway exists even for reading aloud, given that such a route might not be necessary to explain how novel words are pronounced (which is the most obvious rationale for such a route). Evidence against the existence of a nonlexical route to pronunciation is the apparent involvement of word bodies in the generation of phonological representations. On the other hand, evidence in favour of the nonlexical route is the existence of forms of dyslexia where the patterns of reading performance suggest that a nonlexical route has either been selectively impaired or selectively spared. In addition, the preferred pronunciations of nonwords suggest the use of simple rules which are independent of lexical information.

The resolution of this conflict has been to suppose that the lexicon represents words in a hierarchy of different sized sublexical units. These units are both orthographically defined and phonologically defined. The phonological units may or may not be given much weight during lexical processing, depending upon the task requirements. If the task requires overt pronunciation, homophone decision, or a heavy load on verbally coded working memory, then the phonological representation is given more importance than if a simple lexical decision response is required.

In viewing lexical access in this way, the original question of whether or not visual lexical access normally requires the mediation of a phonological representation, becomes rather meaningless. It is no longer a question of whether phonology is important in mediating visual lexical access or whether it is extracted from the lexical entry after access. Instead, phonological representations emerge during the process of lexical access, and are either utilized or not.

Since orthographic information remains the primary basis for lexical access in reading, we now turn to a more detailed examination of the nature of the orthographic access system.

NOTES

1.   In fact, Davelaar, M. Coltheart, Besner, and Jonasson (1978) do find evidence for a homophone effect for low frequency words, although only when there are no pseudohomophones in the experiment.

2.   Parkin (1982) found that irregular words took longer to classify in the lexical decision task, but only when they were "strange" words like YACHT and GAUGE, while Waters and Seidenberg (1985) found a regularity effect in lexical decision for ordinary irregular low frequency words, but only when the experiment included these "strange" words.

3.   It should be noted that most cases of surface dyslexia are not as clear-cut as this. Nevertheless, dual-route theorists have focused on the idealized case presented here (e.g. M.Coltheart, 1985).

4.   The lowest levels would actually consist of graphemic and phonetic feature units. However, these can be ignored for present purposes.

CHAPTER FIVE

Morphographic Processing

In this chapter we will consider whether readers avail themselves of the internal orthographic structure of words, which will be referred to as "morphographic" processing (see Taft, 1985), a term which embraces both morphological structure (i.e. stems and affix morphemes) and orthographic syllabic structure. For example, is the word UNJUSTLY read by separating it into its components (i.e. the morphemes UN, JUST, and LY) and recognizing it through its stem, JUST? What about the word WALRUS? Is it analysed into its syllables, WAL and RUS? In examining this issue of morphographic processing, we will begin by adopting the approach in which the research was originally framed.

MORPHOLOGICAL DECOMPOSITION

Stem Storage and Affix Stripping

The two traditional models of lexical access, the search and logogen models, include (at least) two different types of representations of words. There is the representation found in the input device (peripheral access file or input logogen system), and the representation found in the central device (master file or cognitive system/output logogen system). The former is used in the match with the incoming sensory information, while the latter provides complete information about the word for output purposes. The representation in the input system is required only to provide sufficient information for the appropriate lexical entry to become a candidate for recognition. Therefore, it is not necessary for the input representation to be a representation of the complete word. It was with this idea in mind that Taft and Forster (1975) put forward the concept of stem storage.

It is clear that the word UNJUSTLY is generated from the word JUST, and therefore it is logically sensible that these two words be related in some way in the lexicon; in a way that is different to the relationship between two words which have the same semantic association, but which are not morphologically related (e.g. JUST and UNFAIRLY). Taft and Forster (1975) suggest (based on a similar proposal by Murrell & Morton, 1974) that the affixed word is not actually represented in the input system, but is recognized via access to the representation of its stem. In other words, access to the entry JUST in the input store allows the representation UNJUSTLY to be found in the central lexicon. If this conceptualization of the system is correct, then recognition of an affixed word would require a decomposition of that word into its stem and affixes in order that the stem be made available for use in the sensory-to-lexical match in the input device.

The stem of a suffixed word could logically be isolated via a left-to-right parsing process whereby larger and larger units which begin with the first letter are tested out until the stem is found (e.g. trying out J, JU, JUS, and finally JUST when presented with JUSTLY). However, in order to isolate the stem of a prefixed word the affix must be mentally removed in a process which Taft and Forster call "prefix stripping". Thus, the UN of UNJUST must be skipped over in order for the stem JUST to become available to the input system. This entails that the prefix be recognized, presumably via consultation of a mental list of prefixes.

Now, if prefixes are stripped off prior to lexical access because the first few letters are found in the prefix list, any word which begins with such letters will be decomposed into a putative prefix and stem. This means that stems which are not words in their own right will be just as readily isolated as are stems which are themselves words. So, for example, the word REVIVE will be analysed into RE and VIVE just as the word REPRINT will be analysed as RE and PRINT. This leads to the suggestion, made by Taft & Forster (1975), that nonword stems like VIVE (which is also contained in SURVIVE, CONVIVIAL, VIVID, and VIVACIOUS) are actually represented in the input store. Recognition of the word REVIVE, then, requires that RE be stripped off and VIVE be accessed in the input system, thus allowing the full representation of REVIVE to be found in the central system.

There are other words, however, whose first few letters would be found in the prefix list, but which could not be considered to be prefixed.

For example, the words RELISH, REGATTA, and UNDULATE could neither logically nor intuitively (nor even etymologically) be considered to be prefixed words. Although the prefix stripping process will lead to an attempt to access the putative stems of these "pseudoprefixed words" (i.e. LISH, GATTA, and DULATE), there is no linguistic reason for these stems to be stored in the input system and, therefore, access via this route will fail. It is only when access is attempted using the complete words that the appropriate lexical entries will be found.

Empirical examination of the above theory of morphological decomposition has centred on four different paradigms: nonword interference, pseudoaffixed word recognition, stem frequency, and repetition priming.

Nonword Interference

The nonword interference effect is the same as the word similarity effect introduced in the first chapter. It takes longer to classify a letter string as a nonword the more that letter string is consistent with lexical information. Therefore, if nonword stems, like VIVE, are actually lexically represented (in the sense of being stored in the input system) then they should be difficult to classify as nonwords in a lexical decision experiment compared to pseudostems like LISH which are not lexically represented. This is what Taft and Forster (1975) found. They also report a similar interference effect for word items where words like VENT, which are stems of higher frequency prefixed words (like PREVENT), were found to take longer to recognize than words of the same frequency which are not parts of other words, like COIN. This was taken to be a result of accessing the inappropriate stem representation in the input store. It should also be noted that, in accordance with the search and verification models of lexical access, words which were stems of lower frequency prefixed words did not produce such an interference effect (e.g. CARD from DISCARD).

Evidence for the idea that prefixes are stripped off in order for the stem to be found in the input system came from a further experiment carried out by Taft and Forster. An interference effect was observed with inappropriately prefixed nonwords like INVIVE compared to INLISH. It is only if the item were analysed into a putative prefix and stem that the genuine stem VIVE could lead to a delay in lexical decision times.

Further support for the decomposition model comes from a study by Taft, Hambly, and Kinoshita (1986). Not only did inappropriately prefixed stems like INVIVE take longer to classify than control prefixed nonwords like INVAPE (where VAPE is not part of a real word), but stems with an added nonprefix like IBVIVE took the same amount of time to classify as control nonprefixed nonwords like IBVAPE. In other words, the existence of a stem in the nonword only led to interference when that stem was preceded by a prefix. The VIVE of IBVIVE never appeared to enter the access system since no interference was evident, thus indicating that only letters that form a prefix are stripped off.

Nonword interference effects have been rarely examined in the case of suffixed words. Taft (1985) reports some unpublished work in relation to this issue. Nonword stems of inflected words are very rare (e.g. SUD from SUDS) and have a dubious status as nonwords, and therefore were not examined. However, nonword stems of derived words (e.g. JOLL from JOLLY)[1] were found to take no longer to reject than first syllables of monomorphemic words (e.g. PUZZ from PUZZLE). This result implies that stems of derived words are treated in the same way as first syllables of monomorphemic words, which raises the possibility that first syllables are also represented in the input device. This is an idea which will be pursued later in this chapter. Further, if stems of derived words do not have a special status in the lexical input system, there is no reason for derivational suffixes to be stripped off prior to access. Instead, the stem can be located via the left-to-right parsing procedure outlined earlier.

Pseudoaffixed Word Recognition

As pointed out earlier, a prelexical prefix stripping procedure should lead to delays in recognizing pseudoprefixed words like RELISH. The RE would be skipped over and an unsuccessful attempt made to locate LISH in the input device. The word would only be recognized after an attempt is made to access the undecomposed version of the letter string. If this attempt at accessing the whole word were made subsequent to the failed attempt at accessing the putative stem (rather than in parallel), then delayed recognition times should ensue.

Such a result was obtained by Rubin, Becker, and Freeman (1979), though only when prefixed nonwords were also included in the experiment. They claimed from this that prefix stripping is only employed when the presence of morphologically complex nonwords forces a morphological decomposition strategy. Taft (1981), however, has answered this criticism by demonstrating a delay in naming pseudoprefixed words when nonwords were entirely eliminated from the experiment. The results of Rubin et al. are themselves explained in terms of an experiment-specific strategy, whereby subjects need not access the words in the normal manner when none of the nonwords are prefixed, since the word/nonword discrimination can be based purely on whether or not the stimulus item begins with letters that form a prefix.

While Henderson, Wallis, and Knight (1984) failed to find a pseudoprefix effect, they used only a small number of items (some of which might be considered to be prefixed rather than pseudoprefixed, e.g. ASSENT, SUBLIME). On the other hand, Bergman, Hudson, and Eling (1988) were able to demonstrate a clear delay in lexical decision responses to pseudoprefixed words in Dutch, thus concluding in favour of the prefix stripping model. Using a completely different paradigm, Lima (1987) found that pseudoprefixed words embedded in sentences were given longer eye fixations than prefixed words similarly embedded, hence supporting the idea of prefix stripping during fluent silent reading. Therefore the weight of evidence seems to point to a prelexical morphological decomposition mechanism for prefixed words.

As far as suffix stripping goes, there has been no report of any difficulty in recognizing pseudoderived words, like PANIC, HARNESS, and GARMENT, compared to genuinely derived words or nonderived words (Bergman et al., 1988; Manelis & Tharp, 1977; Smith and Sterling, 1982; Taft, 1985). This result is in line with the conclusions drawn from the lack of interference found with derived nonwords, that is, that derived words are treated no differently to other polysyllabic words.

In seeming contradiction to this, however, both Manelis and Tharp (1977) and Colé, Beauvillain, Pavard, and Segui (1986) observed longer lexical decision times when a genuinely derived word and a pseudoderived word were presented as a pair (e.g. AILMENT GARMENT) compared to when two derived words (e.g. AILMENT PAVEMENT) or two pseudoderived words (e.g. GARMENT VEHEMENT) were presented as a pair. While it is unclear whether this effect resulted from facilitation in the case of the homogeneous pairs or delay in the case of the mixed pairs, it seems to suggest that derived words and pseudoderived words are processed differently. It is possible, however, that the effect of the prime word is not that it influences the parsing process of the following word, but rather, that it biases the decision that the accessed entry is the correct word. In other words, genuinely derived and pseudoderived words may be accessed via the same procedure (e.g. left-to-right parsing), but their structure might be represented differently in the central lexicon. If two words are found from lexical information to have the same morphological structure, the decision that the correct lexical entries have been accessed could be facilitated relative to when the morphological structures do not match.

Interestingly, Colé et al. failed to find the same effect with prefixed words as they did with suffixed words. That is, subjects were no slower when prefixed and pseudoprefixed words were mixed than when they were presented in pairs of the same category. Such a result argues against decision bias being the explanation, since such a bias should hold for prefixed words just as much as for suffixed words. However, if the explanation is not one of decision bias, the conclusion from the study of Colé et al. would be that prefixes are not stripped during access, and that the stems of derived words are represented in the input system in a way that is different to the pseudostems of pseudoderived words (see also Segui & Zubizarreta, 1985, and Colé, Beauvillain, & Segui, 1989). This conclusion is the exact opposite of the one drawn so far in this chapter.

Perhaps there is an interesting unexplored difference between the recognition of French (the language used by Colé et al.) and English. However, it might also be that a different definition of "pseudoprefixed word" has been used in the French and English research. The French research seems to have adopted the view that a word is prefixed if the stem is a meaningful word in its own right and that all other cases are pseudoprefixed words. In other words, REVIVE would be classified as a pseudoprefixed word by this definition, even though English speakers tend to rate it as being prefixed. If this has indeed been the definition adopted in the French research, the failure to find an effect of pseudoprefixation would not be a problem for the prefix stripping model after all, since pseudoprefixed words would actually be prefixed words.

Stem Frequency Effects

If affixed words are accessed via a representation of their stem, one might expect that words which share a stem (e.g. EMPLOY and DEPLOY) will be accessed via the same representation (PLOY) in the input system. It should therefore be the case that the frequency of the stem of an affixed word influences recognition times for that word, and this has been shown to be the case for both prefixed and inflected words in English (Taft, 1979a) as well as inflected words in Italian (Burani, Salmaso, & Caramazza, 1984). For example, DEPLOY has the same frequency of occurrence as DEFLATE, yet the words with which they share their stem differ in frequency; EMPLOY is more frequent than INFLATE. This means that the stem PLOY is more frequently occurring than the stem FLATE. Taft (1979a) found that words like DEPLOY which had high frequency stems were classified as words more rapidly than those like DEFLATE which had lower frequency stems, even though these words were of the same whole-word frequency (i.e. "surface frequency"). Such a result suggests that a prefixed word is recognized via a representation of its stem, and further, that words sharing a stem also share an entry in the input device.

In addition to the stem frequency effect, Taft and Burani et al. observed a surface frequency effect. That is, when stem frequency is held constant, words of high surface frequency (e.g. EMPLOY) take less time to recognize than words of lower surface frequency (e.g. DEPLOY). This surface frequency effect can be explained in terms of the frequency with which the affix combines with the stem in the central lexical system. Thus, it is proposed that frequency has its effects at two loci; a stem frequency effect in the input system and a surface frequency effect in the central system.

An examination of derived words by Bradley (1979) revealed a stem frequency effect for words ending in the productive suffixes NESS, MENT, and agentive ER, but not for those ending in the non-productive ION. These results therefore suggest that derivationally related words are accessed via a shared representation, at least when they have a productive suffix. It was previously claimed that derivational suffixes are not stripped off prior to lexical access, but this does not mean that derived words must be stored in the input system in undecomposed form. It may be that they are stored as stems, but are accessed via a left-to-right parsing procedure. However, having concluded above that the stem of a derived word appears to be represented in the input system no differently to the first syllable of a monomorphemic, polysyllabic word, it is necessary to suppose that if stems are stored in the access system, then so are first syllables. As mentioned earlier, such a proposal will be presented later in the chapter.

Repetition Priming

Another technique that has been employed in the examination of morphological processing in lexical access has been to test whether or not the presentation of a morphological variant of a word facilitates the recognition of that word. For example, if lexical decision times to HAPPY are primed to the same degree by UNHAPPY as they are by HAPPY itself, one could conclude that UNHAPPY and HAPPY share a lexical representation. Such a result was obtained by Stanners, Neiser, and Painton (1979a) using prefixed words, and by Murrell and Morton (1974), Stanners, Neiser, Hernon, and Hall (1979b), and Fowler, Napps, and Feldman (1985) using inflected words. On finding that derived words only partially primed their stem forms (e.g. SELECT was recognized faster when preceded by SELECTIVE than when preceded by an unrelated word, but slower than when preceded by SELECT itself), Stanners et al. (1979b) concluded that a derived word has a separate, although related, lexical representation from its stem. However, Fowler et al. (1985) claim that part of the priming effect is episodic in origin (see also Forster & Davis, 1984) and when this episodic influence is eliminated by a blocking technique, derived words are found to prime their stems to the same degree that inflected words prime their stems. In addition, irregularly affixed words (e.g. SWEPT) behave in the same way as regularly affixed words (e.g. SWEEPING). In agreement with this, Forster et al. (1987) observed a priming effect with irregularly inflected words using a masked priming paradigm.

In order to explain why the nature of the relationship between the morphologically related prime and target words does not influence the extent of the priming effect, Fowler et al. (1985) favour an interactive-activation model which incorporates a set of stem morpheme nodes somewhere between the letter level nodes and the word level nodes. All morphologically related words share a morpheme node, but not a word node. Priming arises from the repeated activation of a stem node and also, in the case of an identical target and prime, the repeated activation of a word node. By this account then, the priming effect using identical primes and targets (e.g. SWEEPING SWEEPING) should be greater than the effect observed with non-identical but morphologically related primes and targets (e.g. SWEEPING SWEEP) since the former involves the repeated activation of an extra node. In point of fact, such a difference in magnitude of priming is rarely observed statistically, although Fowler et al. (1985) claim that it is frequently observed numerically. What Fowler et al. point out to be the greatest hurdle for the activation model, however, is the fact that repetition priming can last for a considerable period of time, which is incompatible with the notion of a temporary maintenance of activation within a node.

It seems then, that there is a strategic component to the form-priming effects observed by Fowler et al., even though they claimed to have eliminated episodic influences from their experiments. So, until we know what the basis of the priming effect is, the conclusions drawn from this paradigm regarding morphological representation in the lexicon must remain tentative.

Alternatives to the Taft and Forster Model

The defining characteristics of the Taft and Forster model are that prefixes are always stripped off prior to access, that stem morphemes participate in the sensory-to-lexical match, and that information about the complete word is obtained from the lexical entry. Taft and Forster use a search model framework, but this is not essential to the basic issue of morphological decomposition. In the activation model supported by Fowler et al. (1985) representations of complete words are accessed through the activation of stem morpheme nodes, and this could simply be seen as an activation interpretation of a morpheme-based input system leading to a word-based central lexical system. Where the activation model crucially differs from the Taft and Forster model is that it does not require prefix stripping in order for the morpheme representation to be activated. The stem node is activated whenever the appropriate combination of letters occurs within the letter string, regardless of whether this combination of letters is preceded by a prefix or not.

There are two lines of evidence that are not consistent with this position. First, it is difficult to see how the delay observed in responding to pseudoprefixed words (Bergman et al., 1988; Lima, 1987; Taft, 1981) could be explained without the notion of inadvertent prefix stripping. In the activation model, a pseudoprefixed word like REGATTA should simply be recognized at the word level without passing through any stem morpheme nodes and thus should not create any problems. Secondly, there is the observation made by Taft et al. (1986) that nonwords which contain a real word stem are associated with delayed lexical decision responses only when the stem is preceded by a prefix. That is, INVIVE takes longer to classify as a nonword than INVAPE, but IBVIVE takes no longer to classify than IBVAPE. The delay in responses to INVIVE could be explained by the activation model in terms of a morpheme node "VIVE" being activated and therefore providing inappropriate activation to the word nodes "REVIVE" and "SURVIVE". However, IBVIVE should do the same thing and hence produce the same delay. It seems therefore that prefix stripping must be incorporated into the Fowler et al. model, and thus the model could simply be seen as an activation version of the Taft and Forster position. However, in a later section we will see that there is a prefix stripping procedure that can be incorporated into an activation model that is different to the procedure outlined by Taft and Forster.

A second alternative to the model, which says that morphological decomposition is obligatory, is the proposal that both whole words and stem morphemes are represented in the lexicon, but morphological decomposition only comes into play when an attempt at whole word access fails. By this account (e.g. Caramazza, Laudanna, & Romani, 1988; Henderson, 1985b; Stanners et al., 1979a), one should only observe effects of morphological decomposition on nonword items. How then does one account for the stem frequency effect and the pseudoprefix effect, which are both obtained using words as items?

Caramazza et al. (1988) propose that, although the sensory-to-lexical matching process takes place using the whole letter string, if it is successful, the entry for the stem of the word becomes activated. Although it is not clear what the purpose of this stem activation is, the stem frequency effect can be explained by saying that activation in the entry for the stem of a word leads to an increase in the resting activation level in all those whole word entries that are linked to that stem (Laudanna & Burani, 1985). Thus the resting level for DEPLOY will be raised whenever the stem PLOY is activated by the accessing of the lexical entry EMPLOY. It is therefore possible to explain the stem frequency effect without resort to the notion of compulsory prefix stripping.

The pseudoprefix effect is accounted for by simply denying that it is genuine (e.g. Henderson et al., 1984; Caramazza et al., 1988). Henderson et al. claim that the stress pattern of the pseudoprefixed words used by Taft (1981) was different to that of the prefixed words used, leading to unusual pronunciations and hence longer naming times. However, such a criticism is unfounded since stress pattern was specifically matched in the Taft experiment, such that there were as many pseudoprefixed words stressed on their second syllable (e.g. DEVOUT, PREDATION) as were prefixed words (e.g. ADVANCE, IMPECCABLE), and as many prefixed words stressed on their first syllable (e.g. RECOGNIZE, INSOLENT) as were pseudoprefixed words (e.g. PRECIPICE, DELUGE).

Caramazza et al. (1988) put their faith in the results of Rubin et al. (1979) which suggest that the pseudoprefix effect might be strategic, while ignoring (though acknowledging) the critique of this study by Taft (1981). In addition, the pseudoprefix effects observed by Lima (1987) and Bergman et al. (1988) need to be explained by any model which supposes that words are recognized without the involvement of morphological decomposition.

Perhaps the strongest evidence against the notion that words are obligatorily accessed via their stem morpheme comes from Andrews (1986). She found that the stem frequency effect for derivationally suffixed words (e.g. BOOKLET versus AILMENT, where BOOK is high frequency and AIL is low frequency) was only obtained when she included other words in the experiment which were clearly polymorphemic, namely compound words like SEAWEED and HANDBOOK. The fact that the stem frequency effect appears to be under strategic control is inconsistent with the notion that the stem frequency effect arises from the nature of a representation that is invariably used to access the suffixed word. While it is not obvious how Andrews results are to be explained (although she favours a vaguely specified model along the lines of that proposed by Fowler et al.), it is clear that the Taft and Forster model, at least in its strongest form, cannot handle them. The real difficulty for the Taft and Forster model lies in Andrews' failure to find a stem frequency effect in her experiment where compound words were not included. It must be pointed out, however, that Bradley (1979) did observe stem frequency effects with derivationally suffixed words in an experiment where no compound words were included, and therefore, it would probably be unwise to accept Andrews result without further investigation.

Compound Word Recognition

The above discussion of morphological decomposition suggests that the stem of a word has an important role to play in word recognition. The strongest characterization of this role, and the one given by Taft and Forster (1976), is to say that the stem is the actual code through which lexical access is achieved. What happens though, when a word has more than one stem, as in the case of a compound word (e.g. SEAWEED)? Does the recognition process centre upon both constituents or does access take place via the first or second constituent alone? According to a model which incorporates a left-to-right parsing process, it should be the case that the first constituent is the lexical access code. Although the second constituent is usually semantically more central to the meaning of a compound word (e.g. SEAWEED is a type of WEED, HANDBOOK is a type of BOOK), it would be difficult for a computational device to isolate the second constituent of a compound word independent of the first constituent. For example, without knowing what the first constituent is, one cannot know whether the second constituent of WIDESPREAD is supposed to be SPREAD, PREAD, READ, or even ESPREAD, whereas a left-to-right parsing procedure will isolate the first constituent, WIDE.

Taft and Forster (1976) addressed this issue using the nonword interference paradigm. Nonwords were composed of either two words (e.g. TOASTPULL), a word followed by a nonword (e.g. SPELLCUNG), a nonword followed by a word (e.g. FLURBPAIR) or two nonwords (e.g. THRIMNADE). It was found that lexical decision times were the same for items like TOASTPULL and SPELLCUNG, as were lexical decisions times for items like FLURBPAIR and THRIMNADE, with the former pair taking longer than the latter pair. In other words, there was a delay in nonword response times when a word appeared as the first constituent, but no delay when a word appeared as the second constituent. Taft and Forster therefore concluded that access takes place via the first constituent only.

It has been noted by Taft (1985) and Andrews (1986), however, that there is a suggestion in the data of an error difference between the word-word items like TOASTPULL and the word-nonword items like SPELLCUNG. There was a 9% error rate for word-word items compared to a 2% error rate for the word-nonword items, which is sizeable but not significant. (The error rates for the nonword-word and nonword-nonword conditions were 5% and 4% respectively.) Added to this, Lima and Pollatsek (1983) found both a reaction time and an error rate difference between word-word and word-nonword items, and these were significant in the analysis of the subject means, although not the item means. A large difference between these two conditions on both reaction time and error rates was also observed by Monsell (1985), but no statistical analysis was reported. It may therefore be the case that the lexical status of the second constituent does come into play when the first constituent is a word.

Further support for this idea comes from Taft (1985) who reports that reversed compounds like BERRYBLACK and WALKJAY are associated with longer and more error-prone lexical decision responses than other word-word compound nonwords like DEMONSHORT and TALLMOP. If only the first constituent were used in access, BERRYBLACK should be rejected as a word when it is determined from the lexical entry for BERRY that BLACK is not a valid ending for BERRY. The existence of the word BLACKBERRY should never come into play since it could only be discovered from the lexical entry for its first constituent BLACK. This account is clearly wrong. The second constituent does provide some sort of access route to the whole compound word.

There is further evidence from other paradigms, using words as items, which seems to support the idea that both constituents are accessed in compound word recognition. Both Taft and Forster (1976) and Andrews (1986) demonstrated an effect on lexical decision times of varying the frequency of the first constituent while holding the overall frequency of the word constant. The effect of varying the frequency of the second constituent was not directly tested. However, when Andrews correlated lexical decision times with frequency, she found the same degree of correlation for the second constituent as for the first constituent.

Interestingly, while words with a high frequency first constituent were faster to recognize than words with a low frequency first constituent, the correlation between frequency and reaction time for the former type of word was a positive one, that is, the higher the frequency of the first (or second) constituent, the longer the reaction time. The explanation for this would seem to lie in some sort of trade-off between the speed of getting to the lexical entry for the constituent and the interference engendered by the competing candidates which share that constituent. Typically, a higher frequency constituent occurs in more compound words than does a low frequency constituent and, therefore, there is the potential for greater interference. For example, while the HAND of HANDBOOK will be accessed more rapidly than the FROST of FROSTBITE, it will also make available more lexical candidates, e.g. HANDWRITING, HANDSHAKE, HANDGUN, HANDMAID, HANDCUFF, etc. which can delay the recognition of HANDBOOK.

What model best explains the fact that both constituents of a compound word seem to play a role in lexical access? According to the Taft and Forster model, one could say that once the lexical entry for the first constituent is accessed, the onset of the second constituent can be determined and therefore the second constituent can be accessed. The only reason for doing this, however, would be if the lexical entry for the second constituent were required for recognition of the compound word to occur, and this is not the case according to the model in its strictest interpretation. One needs to modify the model such that the compound word is not contained within the lexical entry for the first constituent, but rather that both the first and second constituent provide access to the full compound word. Such a modification seems to lead to a model of the type proposed by Fowler et al. and favoured by Andrews.

According to this account, when there is activation of the morpheme node representing either the first or the second constituent, there will be a spread of activation to the unit representing the whole word. It was pointed out earlier, however, that this sort of interactive-activation model cannot explain why the presence of a word stem in a nonword (e.g. INVIVE, IBVIVE) only delays lexical decision times when that stem is preceded by a prefix (Taft et al., 1986). The lexical entry for REVIVE should be activated by the presence of the stem VIVE no matter what other letters surround it. Similarly, the interactive-activation model predicts that FLURBPAIR should activate PAIR and therefore delay lexical decision responses relative to THRIMNADE. Taft and Forster found no sign of a difference between such nonword-word and nonword-nonword items. However, to complicate matters, Monsell (1985) did observe a reaction time difference between items of this type. While it is unclear how to explain this empirical discrepancy,[2] even in Monsell's experiment there is a result that is a challenge for the interactive-activation model.

As in the Taft and Forster experiment, word-nonword items (e.g. SPELLCUNG) were found by Monsell to take longer to respond to than nonword-word items (e.g. FLURBPAIR) and this indicates some form of priority of access to the first constituent. If either constituent were able to activate a lexical node, and if it is activation of an inappropriate lexical node that leads to the interference effect, there would be no reason for there to be less interference when the second constituent is a word than when the first constituent is a word. In order to explain the SPELLCUNG versus FLURBPAIR difference, as well as the INVIVE/INVAPE versus IBVIVE/IBVAPE difference, the model needs to assume some sort of left-to-right parsing such that a failure to find a lexical representation for the first part of the letter string (e.g. FLURB, IB) usually leads to the abandonment of lexical processing. What this amounts to is essentially the Taft and Forster morphological decomposition model, but where the access mechanism is one of activation rather than search. The nodes that represent morphemes are equivalent to the access codes in the orthographic access file, while the nodes representing whole words are equivalent to entries in the lexicon proper. This is the same conclusion that was reached earlier when discussing affixed word recognition. There are, however, several reasons why the activation account can be seen as being preferable to the search metaphor.

First, there is greater flexibility in an activation system, such that it is possible for parts of the letter string other than the first constituent to gain access to the whole word representations. While it seems that activation of the lexical representation for the second constituent typically only occurs when a lexical representation for the first constituent is successfully activated, the nature of the activation system is such that the second constituent (or indeed any other part of the letter string) at least has the potential to activate lexical information.

Secondly, in the Taft and Forster model there needs to be a specific list of prefixes that are consulted prior to access in order to determine whether or not there is anything to strip off. Apart from the fact that there is no independent evidence to support the idea that such a list is available to readers, it is unclear how this model handles combining forms, like BIO, POLY, NEO, etc. which seem to have a linguistic status somewhere between compound word constituents and prefixes. In the activation model, the morphemic lexical nodes can represent any morpheme, be it a stem, prefix, or combining form. When the first few letters of a letter string activate a node that represents a prefix (or combining form), the next letter can be treated as the onset of the next unit to be activated, in the same way that occurs when the first constituent of a compound word activates a lexical node. This is equivalent to prefix stripping. Therefore, the activation account allows one to dispense with the unappealing idea that readers possess a specific listing of prefixes which is available for consultation prior to lexical access.

The one remaining result reported in the morphology literature that was previously said to be a problem for the interactive-activation model, was the delay found in responding to pseudoprefixed words. Once one includes nodes to represent prefixes, this result is no longer a problem. A prefix node will be inappropriately accessed when a pseudoprefixed word is presented and this activation will compete with the activation in the appropriate node (i.e. the node representing the whole monomorphemic word), thus slowing the response time.

It can be seen then that, while compound words make up only a small proportion of the words of English, an examination of how they might be recognized has far-reaching implications for a general account of word recognition.

When talking about compound words, the terms "first constituent" and "second constituent" have been used. It has been further assumed that the important characteristic of these constituents is that they are morphemes. However, it is conceivable that another characteristic of these constituents is also important in lexical access and this is the fact that they are syllables. In the word HANDBOOK, for example, the first constituent HAND is not only the first morpheme, but also the first syllable. We can therefore ask the question: Do syllables play a role in lexical access?

SYLLABLES

Monosyllabic versus Polysyllabic Words

There have been a number of studies which have examined the potential role of syllables in lexical access by directly comparing monosyllabic and polysyllabic words (e.g. Eriksen, Pollack, & Montague, 1970; Forster & Chambers, 1973; Fredriksen & Kroll, 1976; Klapp, 1971; Spoehr & Smith, 1973, Taylor, Miller, & Juola, 1977). The upshot of this research appears to be that the number of syllables does not influence the speed of lexical access, although it is easier to name a monosyllabic letter string than a polysyllabic one, but only when such verbalization is made difficult (see Henderson, 1982; Taft, 1985). However, just because the number of syllables does not appear to affect speed of access, it does not necessarily mean that syllabic analysis is not carried out in lexical access.

For example, if it were the case that words were recognized via access to a representation of their first syllable, a polysyllabic word would actually have an advantage over a monosyllabic word of the same length since its access code would be smaller (e.g. the LANG of LANGUAGE versus the whole word STRAIGHT). This advantage might be counterbalanced, however, by the greater complexity of processing when checking out the rest of the word in the lexicon proper. So, while it may be the case that lexical decision times for polysyllabic words are the same as for monosyllabic words, there is no need to suppose that the two types of word are lexically represented in the same way.

The First Syllable as an Access Code

In order to test whether the first syllable is indeed the code via which lexical access takes place, Taft and Forster (1976) made use of the interference (or word similarity) effect. Their idea was the same as in the interference experiments using affixed words, except that instead of presenting stems of polymorphemic words, like VIVE from REVIVE, they presented first syllables of monomorphemic words like ATH from ATHLETE. What was found was that these first syllable nonwords took longer to respond to than nonwords which were the first part, but not the first syllable of a word (like AWF from AWFUL), which in turn did not differ from nonwords that were not the first part of a word (like ARN). This result was replicated by Taft (1986), and echoed in a similar finding by Manelis and Tharp (1977) who obtained longer lexical decision times to suffixed first syllables (e.g. MURDY from MURDER) than suffixed nonwords (e.g. MALDY). In addition, Taft and Forster (1976) obtained the same pattern of results using words as items, e.g. NEIGH (the first syllable of NEIGHBOUR) took longer to respond to than SHREW (the first part of SHREWD) which did not differ from SCOFF (not part of another word). In agreement with the notion that first syllables are access codes, no interference effect was obtained when final syllables were used, e.g. CULE (from MOLECULE) took no longer to classify as a nonword than SUNE (not part of a word), while BAND (from HUSBAND) took no longer to classify as a word than SEAT (not part of another word).

These findings suggest then, that first syllables are represented in the input system as a means of gaining access to the full information about the word. In accordance with this notion, Manelis and Tharp (1977) observed as much interference in responding to suffixed nonwords when the suffix was attached to a first syllable (e.g. MURDY) as when it was attached to a real monosyllabic word (e.g. LENDY). In other words, the status of MURD in the access system seems to be the same as the status of LEND.

It may appear that the conclusion that words are accessed via a representation of their first syllable is incompatible with the previous conclusion that words are accessed via a representation of their stem morpheme. However, these two ideas can be combined. What one can say is simply that access takes place via a representation of the first syllable of the stem of the word. So, according to this view, the access code for INTREPID would be TREP (as well as for TREPIDATION) and the access code for both TROUBLE and TROUBLESOME would be TROUB. We see, therefore, that the access code for a suffixed word would be the same as for any polymorphemic word, namely a representation of its first syllable.

Definition of Syllable

The syllable has been traditionally defined in pronunciational terms (e.g. Stetson, 1951; Bolinger, 1968; MacKay, 1974), but there is little agreement as to its precise definition particularly in relation to the syllable boundary. Despite the fact that the location of a syllable boundary can vary with the speed with which the word is articulated (e.g. Bell, 1975; Kahn, 1976), it is often assumed (e.g. Hansen & Rodgers, 1968; Spoehr & Smith, 1973) that when the first vowel of a polysyllabic word is long or unstressed, the syllable boundary falls immediately after that vowel (e.g. TI/GER, CI/GAR), that the syllable boundary falls between medial double consonants (e.g. PIS/TOL), and that when the first vowel is short and followed by a single consonant, the boundary falls after that consonant (e.g. BIG/OT). However, this position is by no means universally accepted. For example, a strong case has been made (e.g. Kahn, 1976) for the notion that the same consonant can fall within two adjacent syllables (e.g. PIS/STOL, BIG/GOT) and also for the notion (Anderson & Jones, 1974) that the first syllable includes all consonants following the first vowel (e.g. PIST/OL).

The controversy that exists over the specification of syllable structure appears to cast doubt on the idea that syllables are represented as discrete units in the lexical access system. It would seem unlikely that the access code is the first syllable of a word when linguists are unable to specify what the first syllable actually is. It was partly for this reason that Taft (1979b) put forward the idea of an orthographically defined first syllable: The Basic Orthographic Syllabic Structure or BOSS.

The Basic Orthographic Syllabic Structure (BOSS)

BOSS provides a specification of how a visually presented word can be syllabified without considering its pronunciation. The BOSS is defined as the first part of the (first) stem morpheme of a word up to and including all consonants following its first vowel, but without including an illegal consonant cluster in final position. A consonant cluster is considered to be illegal if it cannot occur in word final position. For example, GL, YC, and TR are all illegal clusters and therefore the BOSS of JUNGLE is JUNG (rather than JUNGL), the BOSS of BOYCOTT is BOY (rather than BOYC), and the BOSS of CENTRAL is CENT (rather than CENTR). Other examples of BOSSes are the THUND of THUNDER, the YEST of YESTERDAY, the TEA of TEAPOT, the SAT of DISSATISFIED, the FIN of FINE, INFINITE, FINAL, and FIN itself.

So, following on from the notion developed by Taft and Forster (1976) that the access code is the first syllable of a word, Taft (1979b) proposed that words are accessed via a representation of their BOSS. The experiments that Taft presented as evidence for the BOSS idea involved the presentation of disyllabic words with their internal structure highlighted in some way. Words were physically split at their BOSS or at their phonological syllable boundary either by means of a gap (e.g. PIST OL versus PIS TOL) or by a change in case (e.g. PISTol versus PIStol). It was found that response times were faster when the words were split after their BOSS than when they were split after their phonological first syllable. However, after Lima and Pollatsek (1983) failed to replicate this finding, Taft (1987) adopted three further paradigms to garner support for the BOSS idea.

In one experiment, words were temporally split by presenting the first part of the word for 200msec prior to presenting the whole word (a technique similar to one used by Lima & Pollatsek), while in a second experiment, words were split by rapidly alternating the first part of the word followed by hatch marks (e.g. THUND##) with the remaining letters of the word preceded by hatch marks (e.g. #####ER) until the subject was able to report what the word was. In the third paradigm, only the first part of the word was presented (e.g. THUND or THUN) and subjects were required to say whether this unit was the beginning of a real word or not. In all three experiments responses were more rapid under the BOSS condition than under the phonological syllable condition.

Words were especially selected for this study so that the first phonological syllable and the BOSS formed the beginning of the same number of words (e.g. THUNDER is the only word beginning with THUN), so that it cannot be said that the BOSS provided fewer competing candidates than did the first syllable. Furthermore, in order to counter the possible criticism that the advantage for the BOSS arose from it simply having more letters than the first syllable, a third condition was introduced into each of the experiments whereby one letter was added to the BOSS (e.g. THUNDE). The fact that this condition was never responded to more quickly than the BOSS condition (and if anything, was responded to more slowly) supported the conclusion that there is indeed something special about the BOSS in lexical access.

While there have been other studies which have produced results which are consistent with the BOSS idea (e.g. Inhoff, 1987; Luszcz, Bungey, & Geffen, 1984; Manelis & Tharp, 1977; Prinzmetal, Treiman, & Rho, 1986), there has been little success beyond Taft's experiments to provide direct support for it. In addition to Lima and Pollatsek, Seidenberg (1987) reports a study which produces data that actually oppose the BOSS notion.

Orthographic Redundancy

Seidenberg (1987) adopted a similar task to that employed by Prinzmetal et al. (1986), whereby a word is presented with its first part printed in one colour and its second in another. The boundary between the two colours might fall either at the BOSS boundary (e.g. between the LAP and EL of LAPEL) or at the phonological syllable boundary (e.g. between LA and PEL). The words were presented tachistoscopically and subjects were asked to say what colour a particular letter was printed in (e.g. the P of LAPEL). It was assumed that if words were processed in accordance with BOSS structure, subjects would incorrectly say that P was the same colour as LA when it was actually the same colour as EL, more often than they would incorrectly say that P was the same colour as EL when it was actually the same colour as LA. In other words, subjects should be more inclined to think that P is connected to LA and therefore the same colour, than to think that it is connected to EL. In the event, however, Seidenberg found the opposite pattern: The second part of the word, PEL, seemed to be treated as a unit, rather than the first part, LAP. On the other hand, when the BOSS and the first syllable coincided, as in SONIC, the favoured unit was the first part of the word, namely SON.

While such a pattern of results might seem to favour the conclusion that word identification is influenced by the word's phonological syllable structure, Seidenberg put forward quite a different interpretation. He proposed that letters which commonly combine together are activated together within an interactive-activation type of framework. There is no syllabification of any sort involved in word recognition; syllable structure is merely a coincidental reflection of orthographic redundancy, whereby, for example, the letters L and A co-occur more often than the letters A and P, and therefore it is LA that emerges as a unit rather than LAP in LAPEL. Similarly, the letters O and N co-occur more often than N and I, and therefore SON emerges as a unit rather than NIC in SONIC. In support of his notion that the colour assignment task reflects orthographic properties rather than syllabic properties of the words, Seidenberg demonstrated the same pattern of results for bisyllabic words (like NAIVE and NAKED) and monosyllabic words of the same orthographic structure (like WAIVE and BAKED).

There are several points, however, which are not consistent with Seidenberg's conclusion. First, while the same pattern of results was obtained for NAIVE as for WAIVE, the pattern actually seems to oppose the notion that letters which commonly occur together emerge as a unit. In particular, the subjects' responses indicate that the I of both NAIVE and WAIVE is more closely connected to the V than to the A. Yet AI is not only an extremely common letter combination, but is likely to form an orthographic unit in the interactive-activation system because of its association with the phonological unit /eɪ/. Similarly, the K of NAKED and BAKED is treated as belonging to ED rather than to NA or BA. Yet the letter combination ED is so common that it should emerge as a unit in its own right (in the same way that LA emerges as a unit in LAPEL). All of the items that are provided by Seidenberg either include a diphthong (as in WAIVE) or a past tense (as in BAKED) and are therefore open to the same criticism.

An experimental result reported by Taft (1987) provides a further problem for the conclusion that orthographic redundancy guides the grouping of letters within a word. Using the temporal priming technique whereby either the BOSS or the phonological first syllable is presented for 200msec prior to the presentation of the whole word, Taft found no significant influence on the size of the BOSS effect from bigram frequency (i.e. the frequency with which two letters combine together in the language). For example, the BOSS of PEWTER is PEWT and the BOSS of VIRTUAL is VIRT, but since WT is a rare bigram and RT is a common bigram, one might expect that PEWT forms a unit less strongly than does VIRT. If this were so, it would be expected that priming VIRTUAL with VIRT would produce faster response times than priming it with VIR, while PEWTER would be no more primed by PEWT than by PEW, and even possibly less primed. The results showed, however, that PEWT primed PEWTER more than PEW did, just as VIRT primed VIRTUAL more than VIR did, and if anything the effect was actually greater for the low bigram frequency items than for the high bigram frequency items. Such a result is hard to reconcile with Seidenberg's position that the only structure that a word possesses that is relevant to lexical access arises from the frequency of its letter combinations.

Just how Seidenberg's results are to be explained, however, is hard to determine. One possibility is to say that there is a general bias in the colour-detection task to respond with the colour of the second half of the word, but that this bias can be overturned when both the BOSS and the phonological first syllable combine to suggest that the first part of the word is a unit, as in SONIC (where subjects tend to respond with the colour of the first part of the word). Of course, such an explanation entails a role for the phonological syllable in word recognition, which is a conclusion that was opposed earlier. However, this role may only arise in a task like tachistoscopic identification, where subjects may be reconstructing what the stimulus was from memory.

A Weaker BOSS Model

Even if it turns out to be the case that the BOSS is an important unit in word recognition, it is not the case that its representation must be characterized as in Taft (1979b). More recently, Taft (1987) has put forward the possibility of a weaker characterization of the BOSS, both in its definition and in the way it might be represented in the lexicon.

A more flexible definition was offered whereby the BOSS is determined on the basis of the letters in the word which appear to combine to form a stem morpheme, even though this may not be true linguistically. For example, because LE is a common ending in English and therefore seems to form a unit at the end of a word, the BOSS of TROUBLE would be taken to be TROUB. Similarly, POWD would be taken to be the BOSS of POWDER because ER forms a unit. However, if a person were to feel that the word POWDER was related to the explosive sound POW (because when something explodes it turns to powder), then that individual might treat POW as being the BOSS of POWDER. In this way, one can never be absolutely sure what the BOSS might be for any particular word, for any particular individual, although the original definition presumably provides a fairly reliable approximation, given that the experiments reported by Taft (1987) demonstrate the primacy of the BOSS using that definition.

In relation to the issue of morphological decomposition discussed earlier in this chapter, an interactive-activation account was put forward as an alternative to the search framework used by Taft and Forster. According to this account, there are both morpheme nodes and whole word nodes, hierarchically organized. Now, it would be possible to add in a further type of node, namely a set of BOSS nodes. So, for example, the word YESTERDAY might be represented by YEST at the BOSS level and YESTER at the morpheme level. Nodes are equivalent to access codes, in that they define the type of sublexical unit whose activation leads to the whole word representation being accessed. In this way, the BOSS is a unit of lexical processing, but, being an activation system, there is the flexibility for letter combinations other than the BOSS to ultimately access the lexical entry for the whole word.

Such flexibility allows one to readily explain a result reported by Taft (1987) where words appeared to be accessed even when their BOSS was disrupted. It was found, for example, that TUSIP took longer to classify as a nonword than TUSAR, the interference arising from the fact that TUSIP is one letter different from TULIP while TUSAR is not one letter different from any word. However, since the BOSS of TULIP (i.e. TUL) is not actually present in TUSIP, such a result is difficult to explain in terms of the strong model which says that words are only accessible through a lexical representation of their BOSS. The interactive-activation model, on the other hand, can explain the result by saying that sufficient activation is generated in the TULIP node to delay responses to TUSIP compared to TUSAR. There is some activation in the TUL node when both TUSIP and TUSAR are presented, but the TULIP node gains extra activation when the stimulus ends in IP. This activation could be fed up from the grapheme level directly, or from a node IP which represents the second orthographic syllable of the word.

So, what is being proposed here is an interactive-activation model with a set of BOSS nodes and a set of morpheme nodes; but we can elaborate on this idea further. In the interactive-activation model described in the previous chapter, there is a set of nodes between the grapheme and whole word level that represents word bodies (e.g. the EST of REST). Integrating this notion with the present version of the model, one could say that this level actually corresponds to BOSS bodies (e.g. the EST of YESTERDAY, WRESTLE, and PESTER, as well as REST). In support of this, a recent experiment conducted in the author's laboratory looking at nonword pronunciations has demonstrated a bias arising from the prior presentation of a word with an irregular BOSS body. For example, COUT is pronounced as /ku:t/ rather than /kaʊt/ more often when it is preceded by ROUTINE than when preceded by COUPON, even though in both cases OU is pronounced as /u:/. The bias only seems to occur when the word and the nonword have the same BOSS body.

Compatible with this view is the finding of Jared and Seidenberg (1990) that polysyllabic words with inconsistently pronounced first syllables (e.g. the RIG of RIGID and RIGOUR) took longer to name than polysyllabic words with consistently pronounced first syllables, and that the consistency of the second syllable showed a weaker effect. The fact that the second syllable showed any effect of consistency might be taken as evidence that the body of the second orthographic syllable is also represented by a node, but is less important in activating the whole word (or concept) node. The body of the first syllable will usually define a smaller set of candidates than will that of the second (e.g. UND versus ER in THUNDER) and would therefore be more informative.

The research which led to the conclusion that word bodies are involved in reading (as outlined in Chapter 4) has almost exclusively focused on monosyllabic words, and therefore, has ignored the issue of how polysyllabic words might be processed. Since monosyllabic words are equivalent to BOSSes (except where there is a silent final E), the change from having a word body level to having a BOSS body level does not effectively alter the conclusions drawn from the work on monosyllabic words.[3]

If one accepts that there is a level of BOSS body nodes, there is actually no need to postulate a separate BOSS level as well. The results which have supported the idea of the BOSS as an access code are entirely compatible with the idea that the body of the BOSS is the access code. For example, a demonstration that THUND primes THUNDER more readily than does THUN, could equally be seen as a demonstration that UND primes THUNDER more readily than does UN. Whether the prior presentation of UND does facilitate responses to THUNDER has not yet been examined.

Priming results obtained by Jordan (1986) might be seen as being explicable within this framework. He demonstrated facilitation in responding to a word whose BOSS was the same as the final letters of the prime word (e.g. MONARCH following LEMON). If bodies of both first and second syllables are represented as nodes, one can say that the ON of LEMON activates the same node as the ON of MONARCH and hence produces priming.

THE INTERACTIVE-ACTIVATION MODEL MODIFIED

What we now have is the interactive-activation model as depicted in Fig. 4.1, but with a morpheme level inserted between the body and concept levels, and where the body level refers to the body of the BOSS rather than the body of the word. There are several implications arising from these modifications that need to be considered.

First, does the morpheme level include monomorphemic words? Since HAND, TREAT, ATHLETE, VITAMIN, and so on, are single morphemes as well as being words, it follows that there should be nodes for all of them. If so, the assumption that words are only represented at the concept level is invalid. Nothing is lost, however, by incorporating a morpheme level that includes all monomorphemic words. The decision as to what word a letter string represents must still arise at the "whole word" concept level, since activation of a morpheme node will not provide this information. For example, the HAND morpheme node will be activated whether the presented word is HAND, HANDS, HANDED, HANDY, HANDBOOK, or UNDERHAND, and therefore, one would need to determine which concept node was the most active in order to determine which of these words was the one that was presented. The appropriate concept node will become more active than any others on the basis of activation passing up from the nodes representing the rest of the word (e.g. the morpheme nodes for ED, BOOK, UNDER, etc.).

Of course, the morpheme node representing the stem of the word will be the most important source of activation, since it will provide the most useful means of narrowing in on the appropriate concept node. Activation coming from the ED morpheme node, for example, would provide activation to a huge number of concept nodes and would therefore play a more useful role in discriminating between the small set of concept nodes that has been activated by the stem. Such a conception of the system is actually not very different to the traditional account, in that it says that all the words which share the stem of the presented item are accessed and that this set is narrowed down with reference to the rest of the item. According to the current proposal, however, access to the words which share the same stem is not a discrete stage that precedes the narrowing down stage, but rather both are part of the general process of activation, with the stem emerging as the most important source of activation.

A second factor that must be considered is whether there are both orthographic and phonological morpheme nodes. It might seem that phonological morpheme nodes are unnecessary given that the pronunciation of morphemes could be determined from the combined pronunciations of sublexical units. However, there is a general problem that arises for the model regarding pronunciation once polysyllabic words are introduced. In particular, even if the pronunciation of the sublexical units of a polysyllabic word can be determined independently, it is difficult to see how the appropriate stress pattern can be assigned to the whole word without there being some type of information about the pronunciation of the whole word (or at least, the stem morpheme). For example, why should stress be assigned to the first syllable of FAMINE, but to the second syllable of POLITE?

There are several possible solutions to this problem. One is to simply say that morpheme units are represented both orthographically and phonologically; but while this is the simplest solution it is also the most redundant. There are other possibilities. It may be the case that sublexical phonological units include reduced vowels (as in the first syllable of POLITE and the second syllable of FAMINE), and when these are activated (on the basis of activation passing down from the concept nodes) they allow the stress pattern of the whole word to be generated (since reduced vowels are never stressed). One problem with this idea though, is that Taft and Hambly (1985) oppose the idea that reduced vowels are lexically represented, on the basis of the finding that reduced vowels tend to be interpreted as full vowels when a spoken word is processed. However, this finding could be interpreted in terms of contamination from the orthographic representation of the word, where the "full" vowel is represented.

Another possibility is that the submorphemic phonological units could be abstract in nature, along the lines suggested by Chomsky and

Halle (1968; see also Taft, 1984). Chomsky and Halle propose that the stress pattern and other phonetic details of a word are predictable from its underlying abstract phonemic representation. There are several drawbacks to this view however. First, abstract phonemic representations are often determined on the basis of the pronunciation of morphologically related words (e.g. the abstract representation of the word SIGN includes a /g/ because a /g/ can be heard in the related word SIGNIFY) and it is difficult to see how this fact could be captured at a submorphemic level of representation. Secondly, the phonological units are supposed to be involved in the recognition of spoken words and therefore they need to be compatible with incoming pronunciations rather than with abstract representations which are not manifested in the pronunciation.

Whatever the appropriate account is, the point has been made that the implications of the necessary inclusion of polysyllabic and polymorphemic words into the interactive-activation system requires careful consideration.

NOTES

1. For a description of the difference between inflected and derived words, see Selkirk (1982). In general, inflectional suffixes alter the tense of a verb or the number of a noun (e.g. ED, ING, S), while derivational suffixes are used to generate one part of speech from another (e.g. Y, NESS, MENT).

2. One factor that was not controlled in either study was the wordlikeness of the overall nonword (e.g. BWEGMAZ is less like a word than is BREGMAL). It may be that this important factor varied between conditions in one or both of the experiments and led to the different pattern of results

3. There will be the occasional cases, however, where the frequency and consistency characteristics of the bodies will be affected. For example, when the body AST occurs in monosyllabic words, it is consistently pronounced by most non-American English speakers as /a:st/ (e.g. BLAST, CAST, LAST, FAST, MAST, etc.) rather than /æst/, but when it occurs as the body of the BOSS, it is sometimes pronounced /æst/ (e.g. DRASTIC, GASTRIC, PASTEL, MASTICATE, etc.) and therefore would be considered to be inconsistent.

CHAPTER SIX

Conclusions and
Future Directions

OVERVIEW

The model that has been developed during the course of this monograph is one where information about the whole word is accessed via the activation of sublexical units ranging from letters, through bodies, to morphemes. Activation passes both up and down the different levels of representation, as well as between orthographic units and phonological units at the same level.

While such an interactive-activation model has been found to be a useful way of conceptualizing the lexical access system, we must not lose sight of the fact that there are still features of the model that are problematical. In Chapter 2 it was pointed that there were difficulties for the model with regard to the method by which the final decision is made that a letter string is a word or not. A pure interactive-activation model incorporates the idea that a lexical unit must be activated to some criterially greater degree than any other before it is accepted as the correct word and that this process is expedited through the inhibition of inappropriate lexical units. We saw, however, that such an account of how the decision is reached fails to adequately explain the delay in response times to nonwords arising from their similarity to real words, and also does not provide a convincing account of semantic priming, given the inhibitory mechanism. The suggested solution to these problems was the proposal of a post-access checking strategy that is brought into play when there is some doubt about the acceptability of the most highly activated word. The accessed word is checked back against the stimulus item to confirm that it matches orthographically. If it does not match, it is classified as a nonword (or recognized as a typesetting or spelling error).

When the letter string is presented within a sentential context, as it usually will be in the reading setting, the context can take over the role of the checking stage. If the accessed word fits in with the context, it can be accepted as readily as when an orthographic check is made. On the other hand, if it does not fit in with the context, an orthographic check is required subsequent to the failed contextual check in case the item is actually a word that is incongruous with the context. Such a process would lead to the inhibition effects reported in Chapter 3, even in the naming task, since one wants to be sure that the right word is being named.

Chapter 4 presented several further empirical concerns, like the *ad hoc* assumptions that are required to explain nonword pronunciations and form-priming, and Chapter 5 highlighted some of the considerations that need to be given when a morphemic level is included in the model. It would seem that further evidence is needed to support the additional assumptions that have been made to explain the empirical data.

THE USE OF SIMULATIONS

One approach that has been used to provide evidence for aspects of the interactive-activation model, is to observe the success of computer simulations using that model (e.g. McClelland & Elman, 1986; McClelland & Rumelhart, 1981). Success is measured by the closeness of correspondence between the time that subjects take to respond to a stimulus word and some measure of the time that the unit representing that word takes to reach a higher activation level than any other units. On the whole, simulations of various aspects of word recognition appear to have been quite successful using the interactive-activation framework.

The fact that a model implemented on the computer appears to accurately simulate human performance can be very seductive support for that model. However, the success of a simulation often merely demonstrates that that particular model does what it is designed to do, rather than providing the correct account of performance. For example, it should be perfectly possible to set up a computer simulation of morphological decomposition within a search framework (e.g. the model of Taft & Forster, 1975) which closely simulates the empirical findings. However, this would merely say that the computer implementation of the model was successful and would add nothing to whether the model is appropriate or not. The latter can only be determined by testing predictions derived from the model; something which can be undertaken with or without the existence of the simulation. On the other hand, a simulation is crucial where the model that one develops cannot be conceptualized independently of its computational implementation. One such model of word recognition has recently been put forward by Seidenberg and McClelland (1989).

A DISTRIBUTED CONNECTIONIST MODEL

The interactive-activation model as discussed so far is a connectionist model whereby the units that are connected to each other represent definable segments of words (e.g. letters, morphemes, etc.). Recently, however, there have been attempts to apply a different type of connectionist model to lexical processing issues. According to this version of the model, there are no "localized" units representing definable word segments. Instead, the identification and pronunciation of a word is mediated by the development of patterns of activation distributed across a large number of units (e.g. Rumelhart & McClelland, 1986; Seidenberg, 1989; Seidenberg & McClelland, 1989).

To broadly summarize the account given by Seidenberg & McClelland (1989), there is a set of orthographic units, a set of phonological units, and a set of "hidden" units which mediate between the orthographic and phonological units. During an initial training phase, the model is exposed to more and more orthographic-phonological pairings (like CLEAN - /kli:n/) and the pattern of activation within the hidden units evolves via a specific learning algorithm (back-propagation). The preferred pronunciation for any subsequently presented letter string is based on the highest output score derived from the pattern of activation generated in the phonological units (as mediated by the pattern of activation in the hidden units). A lexical decision response is based on the amount of discrepancy between the pattern of activation in the orthographic units mediated by the hidden units and the pattern of activation in the orthographic units generated by the letter string itself. The larger the discrepancy, the greater the likelihood that the letter string is a nonword.

While the same hidden units might be involved in the activation pattern for a number of different words, there appears to be no definable pattern of activation specific to a particular type of stimulus item, unlike in the localized interactive-activation model. For example, it is not the case that all words containing a particular body produce a similar pattern of activation within the hidden units, even when that body is pronounced in the same way. This is exemplified by the fact that /mɪ/ is the pronunciation that is preferentially activated when the word MOW is presented, and /kraʊ/ when CROW is presented (according to the list given by Seidenberg and McClelland of the few pronunciation errors made by the model). In addition, morphological and syllabic influences on word recognition are seen in the model as emerging from the pattern of activation within the hidden units. The pattern of activation is influenced by the frequency with which particular letter combinations occur in the training set (although the details of this influence have not been elucidated). There are no specific representations of morphemes or syllables: Their influence on lexical processing arises soley through their prevalence in the language (see discussion of this sort of proposal in Chapter 5).

There are both specific and general criticisms that have been directed against this distributed connectionist model. Specific criticisms have been made by Besner, Twilley, McCann, and Seergobin (1990). They counter the claims made by Seidenberg and McClelland that distributed processing produces pronunciations and lexical decision responses for both words and nonwords in a manner that is similar to human performance. Besner et al. demonstrate that Seidenberg and McClelland's model fails to produce the pronunciations of nonwords which are typically made by human readers, and observe that the model cannot successfully make homophone decisions. In addition, they argue that Seidenberg and McClelland's attempt to explain the delay in lexical decisions made to pseudohomophones in terms of orthographic factors is inadequate. In turn, Seidenberg and McClelland (1990) answer these criticisms saying, amongst other things, that the model would be more accurate in pronouncing nonwords if it were trained on more words, and reaffirming that a genuine pseudohomophone effect does not exist.

Seidenberg (1989) attempts to address some of the more general criticisms that have been directed toward the model. Amongst these is the issue of falsifiability, where the objection is that connectionist models would be able to explain any set of data were one to fiddle with the parameters of the model (e.g. by adjusting the weights given to the connections between units). Seidenberg counters this concern by pointing out how the earlier McClelland and Rumelhart connectionist model is able to be falsified, and claims further that the Seidenberg and McClelland model has very few parameters to manipulate anyway.

A related criticism concerns the ability of the model to make predictions. It would certainly be possible to find two sets of items which differ on the output values generated for them by the model and therefore which would be predicted to differ in the experimental setting. The difficulty for the model arises in determining what those two sets represent and why they should be selected in the first place. In response to such a concern, Seidenberg (1989) makes a specific prediction from the model that he asserts is "nonobvious". He states: "there is a class of nonwords (such as BLUST and RENK) that should be easier to name than low-frequency words (such as FUGUE and TYKE). This would contradict the universal finding that words are named faster than nonwords" (p.64).

Such a statement, however, actually highlights the problem that the model has in making predictions. Can one define, a priori, what class of regular nonwords and lower frequency words will show this effect? Presumably, one needs to find items where the nonwords have higher phonological output scores than do the words. But how does one summarize the source of these higher output scores? A likely candidate for this would be the frequency of sublexical units since TYKE and FUGUE are characterized by unique word bodies. However, body frequency does not seem to be relevant (at least from the examples given) since the ENK of RENK does not occur in English at all. If one cannot be more specific in one's definition of which items should show an effect, the model verges on the untestable. It is no good defining items purely in terms of the actual output values generated by the model, since this is tantamount to saying that an item takes longer to pronounce the more difficult it is to come up with a pronunciation. Furthermore, no other models could be tested against the distributed connectionist model if items were defined in terms of output scores, since such scores are not a feature of any other model.[1] Note, by the way, that the prediction of slower naming times to unusually spelt rare words compared to simple nonwords would be entirely compatible with almost any model. For example, one could explain it in terms of difficulty in applying grapheme-to-phoneme conversion rules, or simply in terms of subjects not being sure of the correct pronunciation.

Even if it were the case that a model could be implemented such that its training with particular stimuli allows it to respond to those stimuli in exactly the same way as a human being does, what would be the value of such a model? As an attempt to get a computer to be an artificial human being, the model would obviously be a success. In addition, it may possibly allow us to say something about the nature of the functioning of the human neural system. But as a means of concretizing a set of abstract ideas such that predictions can be generated in relation to those ideas and such that those ideas can be readily conveyed to others, the model would not be very helpful. The interactive-activation model, search model, etc. are all concrete frameworks for thinking about lexical access; if the perfect distributed processing model were to be developed, we would still need to come up with concrete frameworks to summarize and describe what the distributed processing model was doing. A facsimile of human performance is not an explanatory model of human performance.

It remains to be seen, in the light of the sort of criticisms raised above, what impact the distributed processing model will have on research in the area of lexical access.

PROCESSING IN LANGUAGES OTHER THAN ENGLISH

The final issue to be mentioned concerns the fact that, since the bulk of the research into lexical access has been carried out using English stimuli, what I have talked about has been oriented toward the English language. Does this mean that the lexical processing mechanisms described in this volume are only of relevance to reading in English?

It would seem not. In fact, several studies have been referred to in this volume which used a language other than English. Such languages include Italian (Burani et al., 1984; Caramazza et al., 1988; Laudanna & Burani, 1985; Tabossi, 1988), French (Grainger et al., 1989; Segui et al., 1982; Segui & Zubizarreta, 1985; Colé et al., 1986, 1989), Serbo-Croatian (Lukatela et al., 1983), and Dutch (de Groot, 1983, 1984; Bergman et al., 1988), and there are a number of other studies which have exploited specific characteristics of languages other than English. For example, Lukatela, Gligorijevic, Kostic, and Turvey (1980) and Feldman and Fowler (1987) have made use of the morphological characteristics of Serbo-Croatian, while Günther (1988) has done the same with German. Navon and Shimron (1981) and Frost, Katz, and Bentin (1987) have explored the implications of the fact that Hebrew need not include vowels in its script, while Frost et al. (1987), Frost and Katz (1989), and Katz and Feldman (1983) have compared responses to English and Serbo-Croatian, where the latter has a much more highly predictable spelling-to-sound relationship than the former. While it seems from these studies that specific details of the lexical mechanism may be influenced by the specific characteristics of the language being examined, the same general framework seems to be applicable to all those studies. For example, Frost and Katz come out in favour of an interactive-activation model that accommodates the results that have been obtained using both English and Serbo-Croatian materials.

Even more impressive, perhaps, are indications that lexical processing in a language with a nonalphabetic orthographic system, namely, Chinese, may be accommodated by a similar model to that which is applied to lexical processing in an alphabetic orthography. For example, whereas grapheme-to-phoneme correspondences are nonexistent in Chinese, there is evidence that some of the phonological effects that are observed in reading English are also observed in reading Chinese (e.g. Cheng & Shih, 1988; Fang, Horng, & Tzeng, 1986; Hung & Tzeng, 1981; Seidenberg, 1985). An interactive-activation model of the sort presented in Chapter 4 is able to account for these results where there are sublexical units translating orthography into phonology which, in Chinese, would represent the subcomponents of characters (phonetic radicals) which provide some information about pronunciation.

In the long run, the model of lexical processing that one adopts should be able to accommodate reading performance in any of the world's written languages, since the reading task, while culturally imposed, must be carried out with the use of cognitive mechanisms which every human being possesses.

NOTE

1. A further problem is that all experiments would need to be designed on the basis of that particular instantiation of the model. Should the model then be modified in any way, for example by increasing the size of the training set, the output scores would change and all the experiments would need to be redesigned.

References

Aitchison, J. (1987). *Words in the mind: An introduction to the mental lexicon.* Oxford: Basil Blackwell Ltd.

Anderson, J. & Jones, C. (1974). Three theses concerning phonological representations. *Journal of Linguistics, 10,* 1-26.

Andrews, S. (1982). Phonological recoding: Is the regularity effect consistent? *Memory & Cognition, 10,* 565-575.

Andrews, S. (1986). Morphological influences on lexical access: Lexical or nonlexical effects? *Journal of Memory and Language, 25,* 726-740.

Andrews, S. (1987). *Word frequency effects: Within or between lexical representations?* Paper presented at the 14th Experimental Psychology Conference, University of New England, N.S.W., Australia, 12–14 May.

Andrews, S. (1989). Frequency and neighbourhood effects on lexical access: Activation or search? *Journal of Experimental Psychology: Learning, Memory, and Cognition, 15,* 802-814.

Antos, S.J. (1979). Processing facilitation in a lexical decision task. *Journal of Experimental Psychology: Human Perception and Performance, 5,* 527-545.

Baddeley, A.D., Eldridge, M., & Lewis, V. (1981). The role of subvocalization in reading. *Quarterly Journal of Experimental Psychology, 33A,* 439-454.

Balota, D.A. & Chumbley, J.I. (1984). Are lexical decisions a good measure of lexical access? The role of word-frequency in the neglected decision stage. *Journal of Experimental Psychology: Human Perception and Performance, 10,* 340-357.

Balota, D.A. & Chumbley, J.I. (1985). The locus of word-frequency effects in the pronunciation task: Lexical access and/or production? *Journal of Memory and Language, 24,* 89-106.

Baron, J. (1973). Phonemic stage not necessary for reading. *Quarterly Journal of Experimental Psychology, 25,* 241-246.

Baron, J. & Strawson, C. (1976). Use of orthographic and word-specific knowledge in reading words aloud. *Journal of Experimental Psychology: Human Perception and Performance, 2*, 386-393.

Baron, J., Treiman, R., Freyd, J., & Kellman, P. (1980). Spelling and reading by rules. In U. Frith (Ed.), *Cognitive processes in spelling*. London: Academic Press.

Becker, C.A. (1976). Allocation of attention during visual word recognition. *Journal of Experimental Psychology: Human Perception and Performance, 2*, 556-566.

Becker, C.A. (1979). Semantic context and word frequency effects in visual word recognition. *Journal of Experimental Psychology: Human Perception and Performance, 5*, 252-259.

Becker, C.A. (1980). Semantic context effects in visual word recognition: An analysis of semantic strategies. *Memory & Cognition, 8*, 493-512.

Becker, C.A. (1985). What do we really know about semantic context effects during reading? In D. Besner, T.G. Waller, & G.E. MacKinnon (Eds.), *Reading research: Advances in theory and practice, Vol. V*. Academic Press, New York.

Becker, C.A. & Killion, T.H. (1977). Interaction of visual and cognitive effects in word recognition. *Journal of Experimental Psychology: Human Perception and Performance, 3*, 389-401.

Bell, A. (1975). *If speakers can't count syllables, what can they do?* Paper presented at the Indiana University Linguistics Circle.

Bergman, M.W., Hudson, P.T.W., & Eling, P.A.T.M. (1988). How simple complex words can be: Morphological processing and word representations. *Quarterly Journal of Experimental Psychology, 40A*, 41-72.

Besner, D. (1983). Basic decoding components in reading: Two dissociable feature extraction processes. *Canadian Journal of Psychology, 37*, 429-438.

Besner, D. & Davelaar, E. (1982). Basic processes in reading: Two phonological codes. *Canadian Journal of Psychology, 36*, 701-711.

Besner, D. & Davelaar, E. (1983). Suedohomofoan effects in visual word recognition: Evidence for phonological processing. *Canadian Journal of Psychology, 37*, 300-305.

Besner, D. & McCann, R.S. (1987). Word frequency and pattern distortion in visual word identification and production: An examination of four classes of models. In M. Coltheart (Ed.), *Attention and performance, XII*. London: Lawrence Erlbaum Associates Limited.

Besner, D., Davies, J., & Daniels, S. (1981). Reading for meaning: The effects of concurrent articulation. *Quarterly Journal of Experimental Psychology, 33A*, 415-437.

Besner, D., Dennis, I., & Davelaar, E. (1985). Reading without phonology? *Quarterly Journal of Experimental Psychology, 37A*, 477-491.

Besner, D., Twilley, L., McCann, R.S., & Seergobin, K. (1990). On the connection between connectionism and data: Are a few words necessary? *Psychological Review, 97*, 432-446.

Bleasdale, F.A. (1983). Paivio's dual-coding model of meaning revisited. In J.C. Yuille (Ed.), *Imagery, memory, and cognition*. Hillsdale, N.J.: Lawrence Erlbaum Associates Inc.

Bleasdale, F.A. (1987). Concreteness-dependent associative priming: Separate lexical organization for concrete and abstract words. *Journal of Experimental Psychology: Learning, Memory, and Cognition, 13*, 582-594.

Bodi, A. (1977). *Semantic priming effects in sentences*. Unpublished honours thesis, Department of Psychology, Monash University, Australia.

Bolinger, D. (1968). Aspects of language. New York: Harcourt.

Bradley, D.C. (1978). *Computational distinctions of vocabulary type*. Unpublished Ph.D. dissertation, MIT.

Bradley, D.C. (1979). Lexical representation of derivational relation. In M. Aronoff & M.L. Kean (Eds.), *Juncture*. Cambridge, Mass: MIT Press.

Brown, G.D. (1987). Resolving inconsistency: A computational model of word naming. *Journal of Memory and Language, 26*, 1-23.

Brown, P. & Besner, D. (1987). The assembly of phonology in oral reading: A new model. In M. Coltheart (Ed.), *Attention and performance, XII*, London: Lawrence Erlbaum Associates Limited.

Bub, D., Cancelliere, A., & Kertesz, A. (1985). Whole-word and analytic translation of spelling to sound in a non-semantic reader. In K.E. Patterson, J.C. Marshall, & M. Coltheart (Eds.), *Surface dyslexia*. London: Lawrence Erlbaum Associates Limited.

Burgess, C., Tanenhaus, M.K., & Seidenberg, M.S. (1989). Context and lexical access: Implications of nonword interference for lexical ambiguity resolution. *Journal of Experimental Psychology: Learning, Memory, and Cognition, 15*, 620-632.

Burani, C., Salmaso, D., & Caramazza, A. (1984). Morphological structure and lexical access. *Visible Language, 18*, 342-352.

Cairns, H.S. & Kamerman, J. (1975). Lexical information processing during sentence comprehension. *Journal of Verbal Learning and Verbal Behavior, 14*, 170-179.

Caramazza, A., Laudanna, A., & Romani, C. (1988). Lexical access and inflectional morphology. *Cognition, 28*, 297-332.

Carpenter, P.A. & Daneman, M. (1981). Lexical retrieval and error recovery in reading: A model based on eye fixations. *Journal of Verbal Learning and Verbal Behavior, 20*, 137-160.

Carroll, J.B., Davies, P., & Richman, B. (1971). *The American Heritage word frequency book*. Boston: Houghton-Mifflin.

Chambers, S.M. (1979). Letter and order information in lexical access. *Journal of Verbal Learning and Verbal Behavior, 18*, 225-241.

Cheng, C.-M. & Shih, S.-I. (1988). The nature of lexical access in Chinese: Evidence from experiments on visual and phonological priming in lexical judgment. In I.-M. Liu. H.-C. Chen, & M.-J. Chen (Eds.), *Cognitive aspects of the Chinese language, Vol. 1*. Hong Kong: Asia Research Service.

Chomsky, N. & Halle, M. (1968). *The sound pattern of English*. New York: Harper & Row.

Chumbley, J.I. & Balota, D.A. (1984). A word's meaning affects the decision in lexical decision. *Memory & Cognition, 12*, 590-606.

Clark, H.H. (1973). The language-as-fixed-effect fallacy:A critique of language statistics in psychological research. *Journal of Verbal Learning and Verbal Behavior, 12*, 335-359.

Clarke, R. & Morton, J. (1983). Cross modality facilitation in tachistoscopic word recognition. *Quarterly Journal of Experimental Psychology, 35A*, 79-96.

Colé, P., Beauvillain, C., Pavard, B., & Segui, J. (1986). Organisation morphologique et accès au lexique. *L'Année Psychologique, 86*, 349-365.

Colé, P., Beauvillain, C., & Segui, J. (1989). On the representation and processing of prefixed and suffixed derived words: A differential frequency effect. *Journal of Memory and Language, 28*, 1-13.

Colombo, L. (1986). Activation and inhibition with orthographically similar words. *Journal of Experimental Psychology: Human Perception and Performance, 12*, 226-234.

Coltheart, M. (1978). Lexical access in simple reading tasks. In G. Underwood (Ed.), *Strategies of information processing*. London: Academic Press.

Coltheart, M. (1980). Reading, phonological recoding and deep dyslexia. In M.Coltheart, K. Patterson, & J.C. Marshall (Eds.), *Deep dyslexia*. London: Routledge & Kegan Paul.

Coltheart, M. (1985). Cognitive neuropsychology and the study of reading. In M.I. Posner & S.M. Marin (Eds.), *Attention and performance, XI*. Hillsdale, N.J.: Lawrence Erlbaum Associates Inc.

Coltheart, M., Davelaar, E. Jonasson, J.T., & Besner, D. (1977). Access to the internal lexicon. In S. Dornic (Ed.), *Attention and performance, VI*. New York: Academic Press.

Coltheart, M., Besner, D., Jonasson, J.T., & Davelaar, E. (1979). Phonological encoding in the lexical decision task. *Quarterly Journal of Experimental Psychology, 31*, 489-507.

Coltheart, M., Patterson, K., & Marshall, J.C. (1980). *Deep dyslexia*. London: Routledge & Kegan Paul.

Coltheart, M., Masterson, J., Byng, S., Prior, M., & Riddoch, J. (1983). Surface dyslexia. *Quarterly Journal of Experimental Psychology, 35A*, 469-495.

Coltheart, V., Laxon, V., Rickard, M., & Elton, C. (1988). Phonological recoding in reading for meaning by adults and children. *Journal of Experimental Psychology: Learning, Memory, and Cognition, 14*, 387-397.

Conrad, C. (1974). Context effects in sentence comprehension: A study of the subjective lexicon. *Memory & Cognition, 2*, 130-138.

Davelaar, E., Coltheart, M., Besner, D., & Jonasson, J.T. (1978). Phonological recoding and lexical access. *Memory & Cognition, 6*, 391-402.

de Groot, A. M. B. (1983). The range of automatic spreading activation in word priming. *Journal of Verbal Learning and Verbal Behavior, 22*, 417-436.

de Groot, A. M. B. (1984). Printed lexical decision: Combined effects of the proportion of related prime-target pairs and the stimulus-onset asynchrony. *Quarterly Journal of Experimental Psychology, 36A*, 253-280.

Dennis, I., Besner, D., & Davelaar, E. (1985). Phonology in visual word recognition: Their is more two this than meats the I. In D. Besner, T.G. Waller, & G.E. MacKinnon (Eds.), *Reading research: Advances in theory and practice, Vol. V*. New York: Academic Press.

Dobbs, A.R., Friedman, A., & Lloyd, J. (1985). Frequency effects in lexical decisions: A test of the verification model. *Journal of Experimental Psychology: Human Perception and Performance, 11*, 81-92.

Ellis, A.W. (1988). *Human cognitive neuropsychology*. Hove: Lawrence Erlbaum Associates Limited.

Eriksen, C.W., Pollack, M.D., & Montague, W.E. (1970). Implicit speech: Mechanism in perceptual encoding? *Journal of Experimental Psychology, 84*, 502-507.

Fang, S.-P., Horng, R.-Y., & Tzeng, O. J.-L. (1986). consistency effects in the Chinese character and pseudo-character naming tasks. In H.S.R. Kao & R. Hoosain (Eds.), *Linguistics, psychology, and the Chinese language*. Centre of Asian Studies: University of Hong Kong.

Feldman, L.B. & Fowler, C.A. (1987). The inflected noun system in Serbo-Croatian: Lexical representation of morphological structure. *Memory & Cognition, 15*, 1-12.

Fischler, I. (1977). Associative facilitation without expectancy in a lexical decision task. *Journal of Experimental Psychology: Human Perception and Performance, 3*, 18-26.

Fischler, I. & Bloom, P. A. (1979). Automatic and attentional processes in the effects of sentence contexts on word recognition. *Journal of Verbal Learning and Verbal Behavior, 18*, 1-20.

Fischler, I. & Goodman, G.O. (1978). Latency of associative activation in memory. *Journal of Experimental Psychology: Human Perception and Performance, 4*, 455-470.

Forbach, G., Stanners, R., & Hochhaus, L. (1974). Repetition and practice effects in a lexical decision task. *Memory & Cognition, 2*, 337-339.

Forster, K.I. (1976). Accessing the mental lexicon. In E.C.J. Walker & R.J. Wales (Eds.), *New approaches to language mechanisms*. Amsterdam: North-Holland.

Forster, K.I. (1979). Levels of processing and the structure of the language processor. In W.E. Cooper & E. Walker (Eds.), Sentence processing. Hillsdale, N.J.: Lawrence Erlbaum Associates Limited.

Forster, K.I. (1981). Priming and the effects of sentence and lexical context on naming time: Evidence for autonomous lexical processing. *Quarterly Journal of Experimental Psychology, 33A*, 465-495

Forster, K.I. (1987). Form-priming with masked primes: The best match hypothesis. In M. Coltheart (Ed.), *Attention and performance, XII*. London: Lawrence Erlbaum Associates Limited.

Forster, K.I. (1989). Basic issues in lexical processing. In W. Marslen-Wilson (Ed.), *Lexical representation and process*. Cambridge, Mass.: MIT Press.

Forster, K.I. & Bednall, E.S. (1976). Terminating and exhaustive search in lexical access. *Memory & Cognition, 4*, 53-61.

Forster, K.I. & Chambers, S.M. (1973). Lexical access and naming time. *Journal of Verbal Learning and Verbal Behavior, 12*, 627-635.

Forster, K.I. & Davis, C. (1984). Repetition priming and frequency attenuation in lexical access. *Journal of Experimental Psychology: Learning, Memory and Cognition, 10*, 680-698.

Forster, K.I., Davis, C., Schoknecht, C., & Carter, R. (1987). Masked priming with graphemically related forms: Repetition or partial activation? *Quarterly Journal of Experimental Psychology, 39A*, 211-251.

Foss, D.J. (1970). Some effects of ambiguity upon sentence comprehension. *Journal of Verbal Learning and Verbal Behavior, 9*, 699-706.

Foss, D.J. (1982). A discourse on semantic priming. *Cognitive Psychology, 14*, 590-607.

Fowler, C.A., Napps, S.E., & Feldman, L. (1985). Relations between regular and irregular morphologically related words in the lexicon as revealed by repetition priming. *Memory & Cognition, 13*, 241-255.

Frauenfelder, U.H. & Tyler, L.K. (1987). *Spoken word recognition*. Cambridge, Mass: MIT Press.

Fredriksen, J.R. & Kroll, J.F. (1976). Spelling and sound: Approaches to the internal lexicon. *Journal of Experimental Psychology: Human Perception and Performance, 2*, 361-379.

Friederici, A.D. (1985). Levels of processing and vocabulary types: Evidence from on-line comprehension in normals and agrammatics. *Cognition, 19*, 133-166.

Frost, R. & Katz, L. (1989). Orthographic depth and the interaction of visual and auditory processing in word recognition. *Memory & Cognition, 17*, 302-310.

Frost, R., Katz, L., & Bentin, S. (1987). Strategies for visual word recognition and orthographical depth: A multilingual comparison. *Journal of Experimental Psychology: Human Perception and Performance, 13*, 104-114.

Funnell, E. (1983). Phonological processes in reading: New evidence from acquired dyslexia. *British Journal of Psychology, 74*, 159-180.

Gernsbacher, M.A. (1984). Resolving 20 years of inconsistent interactions between lexical familiarity and orthography, concreteness, and polysemy. *Journal of Experimental Psychology: General, 113*, 256-281.

Gibson, E.J. (1970). The ontogeny of reading. *American Psychologist, 25*, 136-143.

Glucksberg, S., Kreuz, R.J., & Rho, S. (1986). Context can constrain lexical access: Implications for models of language comprehension. *Journal of Experimental Psychology: Learning, Memory, and Cognition, 12*, 323-335.

Glushko, R.J. (1979). The organization and activation of orthographic knowledge in reading aloud. *Journal of Experimental Psychology: Human Perception and Performance, 5*, 674-691.

Goodman, G.O., McClelland, J.L., & Gibbs, R.W., Jr. (1984). The role of syntactic context in word recognition. *Memory & Cognition, 9*, 580-586.

Gordon, B. & Caramazza, A. (1982). Lexical decision for open-and closed-class words: Failure to replicate frequency sensitivity. *Brain and Language, 15*, 143-160.

Gordon, B. & Caramazza, A. (1983). Closed-and open-class lexical access in agrammatic and fluent aphasics. *Brain and Language, 19*, 335-345.

Gordon, B., & Caramazza, A. (1985). Lexical access and frequency sensitivity: Frequency saturation and open/closed class equivalence. *Cognition, 21*, 95-115.

Gough, P.B. (1972). One second of reading. In J.P.Kavanagh & I.G. Mattingly (Eds.), *Language by eye and by ear*. Cambridge, Mass.: MIT Press.

Grainger, J., O'Regan, J.K., Jacobs, A.M., & Segui, J. (1989). On the role of competing word units in visual word recognition: The neighbourhood frequency effect. *Perception & Psychophysics, 45*, 189-195.

Günther, H. (1988). Oblique word forms in visual word recognition. *Linguistics, 26*, 583-600.

Hansen, D. & Rodgers, T.S. (1968). An exploration of psycholinguistic units in initial reading. In K.S. Goodman (Ed.), *The psycholinguistic nature of the reading process*. Detroit: Wayne State University Press.

Hardyck, C.D., & Petrinovich, L.F. (1970). Subvocal speech and comprehension level as a function of the difficulty level of reading material. *Journal of Verbal Learning and Verbal Behavior, 9*, 647-652.

Henderson, L. (1982). *Orthography and word recognition in reading*. New York: Academic Press.

Henderson, L. (1985a). Issues in the modelling of pronunciation assembly in normal reading. In K.E. Patterson, J.C. Marshall, & M. Coltheart (Eds.), *Surface dyslexia*. London: Lawrence Erlbaum Associates Limited.

Henderson, L. (1985b). Towards a psychology of morphemes. In A.W. Ellis (Ed.), *Progress in the psychology of language, Vol. 1*. London: Lawrence Erlbaum Associates Limited.

Henderson, L., Wallis, J., & Knight, D. (1984). Morphemic structure and lexical access. In H. Bouma & D. Bouwhuis (Eds.), *Attention and performance, X*. London: Lawrence Erlbaum Associates Limited.

Hillinger, M.L. (1980). Priming effects with phonemically similar words: The encoding-bias hypothesis reconsidered. *Memory & Cognition, 8*, 115-123.

Hogaboam, T.W. & Perfetti, C.A. (1975). Lexical ambiguity and sentence comprehension. *Journal of Verbal Learning and Verbal Behavior, 14*, 265-274.

Holley-Wilcox, P. & Blank, M.A. (1980). Evidence for multiple access in the processing of isolated words. *Journal of Experimental Psychology: Human Perception and Performance, 6*, 75-84.

Holmes, V.M. (1979). Accessing ambiguous words during sentence comprehension. *Quarterly Journal of Experimental Psychology, 44*, 13-35.

Humphreys, G.W. & Evett, L.J. (1985). Are there independent lexical and nonlexical routes in word processing? An evaluation of the dual route theory of reading. *The Behavioral and Brain Sciences, 8*, 689-740.

Humphreys, G.W., Evett, L.J., & Taylor, P.E. (1982). Automatic phonological priming in visual word recognition. *Memory & Cognition, 10*, 576-590.

Hung, D.L. & Tzeng, O.J.-L. (1981). Orthographic variations and visual information processing. *Psychological Bulletin, 90*, 377-414.

Inhoff, A.W. (1987). Parafoveal word perception during eye fixations in reading: Effects of visual salience and word structure. In M. Coltheart (Ed.), *Attention and performance, XII*. London: Lawrence Erlbaum Associates Limited.

Inhoff, A.W. & Rayner, K. (1986). Parafoveal word processing during eye fixations in reading: Effects of word frequency. *Perception & Psychophysics, 40*, 431-439.

James, C.T. (1975). The role of semantic information in lexical decisions. *Journal of Experimental Psychology: Human Perception and Performance, 1*, 130-136.

Jared, D. & Seidenberg, M.S. (1990). Naming multisyllabic words. *Journal of Experimental Psychology: Human Perception and Performance, 16*, 92-105.

Jastrzembski, J.E. (1981). Multiple meanings, number of related meanings, frequency of occurrence, and the lexicon. *Cognitive Psychology, 13*, 278-305.

Jastrzembski, J.E. & Stanners, R.F. (1975). Multiple word meanings and lexical search speed. *Journal of Verbal Learning and Verbal Behavior, 14*, 634-637.

Jordan, T.C. (1986). Testing the BOSS hypothesis: Evidence for position-insensitive orthographic priming in the lexical decision task. *Memory & Cognition, 14*, 523-532.

Just, M.A. & Carpenter, P.A. (1980). A theory of reading: From eye fixations to comprehension. *Psychological Review, 87*, 329-354.

Just, M.A. & Carpenter, P.A. (1987). *The psychology of reading and language comprehension*. Boston: Allyn and Bacon.

Kahn, D. (1976). *Syllable-based generalizations in English phonology*. Unpublished Ph.D. thesis, Massachusetts Institute of Technology.

Katz, L. & Feldman, L.B. (1983). Relation between pronunciation and recognition of printed words in deep and shallow orthographies. *Journal of Experimental Psychology: Learning, Memory, and Cognition, 9,* 157-166.

Kay, J. & Bishop, D. (1987). Anatomical differences between nose, palm, and foot, or, the body in question: Further dissection of the processes of sub-lexical spelling-sound translation. In M. Coltheart (Ed.), *Attention and performance, XII.* London: Lawrence Erlbaum Associates Limited.

Kay, J. & Marcel, A. J. (1981). One process, not two, in reading aloud: Lexical analogies do the work of nonlexical rules. *Quarterly Journal of Experimental Psychology, 33A,* 397-414.

Kiger, J.I. & Glass, A.L. (1983). The facilitation of lexical decisions by a prime occurring after the target. *Memory & Cognition, 11,* 356-365.

Kinoshita, S. (1984). *The role of sentence context in recognizing visually confusable words.* Paper presented at the 11th Experimental Psychology Conference, Deakin University, Australia, 18–20 May.

Kinoshita, S. (1985). Sentence context effects on lexically ambiguous words: Evidence for a postaccess inhibition process. *Memory & Cognition, 13,* 579-595.

Kinoshita, S. (1987). Case alternation effect: Two types of word recognition. *Quarterly Journal of Experimental Psychology, 39A,* 701-720.

Kinoshita, S., Taft, M., & Taplin, J.E. (1985). Nonword facilitation in a lexical decision task. *Journal of Experimental Psychology: Learning, Memory, and Cognition, 11,* 346-362.

Kirsner, K. & Smith, M.C. (1974). Modality effects in word recognition. *Memory & Cognition, 2,* 637-640.

Klapp, S.T. (1971). Implicit speech inferred from response latencies in same-different decisions. *Journal of Experimental Psychology, 91,* 262-267.

Kleiman, G.M. (1975). Speech recoding in reading. *Journal of Verbal Learning and Verbal Behavior, 14,* 323-339.

Kolk, H.H.J. & Blomert, L. (1985). On the Bradley hypothesis concerning agrammatism—the nonword interference effect. *Brain and Language, 26,* 94-105.

Koriat, A. (1981). Semantic facilitation in lexical decision as a function of prime-target association. *Memory & Cognition, 9,* 587-598.

Kroll, J.F., & Merves, J.S. (1986). Lexical access for concrete and abstract words. *Journal of Experimental Psychology: Learning, Memory, & Cognition, 12,* 92-107.

Kučera, H. & Francis, W.N. (1967). *Computational analysis of present-day American English.* Providence, R.I.: Brown University Press.

Laudanna, A. & Burani, C. (1985). Address mechanisms to decomposed lexical entries. *Linguistics, 23,* 775-792.

Laxon, V.J., Coltheart, V., & Keating, C. (1988). Children find friendly words friendly too: Words with many orthographic neighbours are easier to read and spell. *British Journal of Educational Psychology, 58,* 103-109.

Levy, B.A. (1977). Speech and meaning processes. *Journal of Verbal Learning and Verbal Behavior, 96,* 623-628.

Lima, S.D. (1987). Morphological analysis in sentence reading. *Journal of Memory & Language, 26,* 84-99.

Lima, S.D. & Pollatsek, A. (1983). Lexical access via an orthographic code? The Basic Orthographic Syllabic (BOSS) reconsidered. *Journal of Verbal Learning and Verbal Behavior, 22,* 310-332.

Lorch, R.F., Jr., Balota, D.A., & Stamm, E.G. (1986). Locus of inhibition effects in the priming of lexical decisions: pre- or postlexical access? *Memory & Cognition, 14*, 95-103.

Lucas, M. (1987). Frequency effects on the processing of ambiguous words in sentence contexts. *Language and Speech, 30*, 25-46.

Lukatela, G., Gligorijevic, B., Kostic, A., & Turvey, M.T. (1980). Representation of inflected nouns in the internal lexicon. *Memory & Cognition, 8*, 415-423.

Lukatela, G., Kostic, A., Feldman, L.B., & Turvey, M.T. (1983). Grammatical priming of inflected nouns. *Memory & Cognition, 11*, 59-63.

Luszcz, M.A., Bungey, J., & Geffen, G. (1984). Orthographic-morphemic factors in reading: A developmental study. *Australian Journal of Psychology, 36*, 355-365.

MacKay, D.G. (1974). Aspects of the syntax of behavior: Syllable structure and speech rate. *Quarterly Journal of Experimental Psychology, 26*, 642-657.

Manelis, L. & Tharp, D.A. (1977). The processing of affixed words. *Memory & Cognition, 4*, 53-61.

Marslen-Wilson, W.D. & Tyler, L.K. (1980). The temporal structure of spoken language understanding. *Cognition, 8*, 1-71.

Martin, M. (1978). Speech recoding in silent reading. *Memory & Cognition, 6*, 108-114.

Martin, R.C. (1982). The pseudohomophone effect: The role of visual similarity in nonword decisions. *Quarterly Journal of Experimental Psychology, 34A*, 395-409.

Mason, M. (1978). Print to sound in mature readers as a function of reader ability and two forms of orthographic redundancy. *Memory & Cognition, 6*, 568-581.

Matthei, E.H. & Kean, M-L. (1989). Postaccess processes in the open vs closed class distinction. *Brain and Language, 36*, 163-180.

McCann, R.S. & Besner, D. (1987). Reading pseudohomophones: Implications for models of pronunciation assembly and the locus of word frequency effects in naming. *Journal of Experimental Psychology: Human Perception and Performance, 13*, 13-24.

McCann, R.S., Besner, D., & Davelaar, E. (1988). Word recognition and identification: Do word-frequency effects reflect lexical access? *Journal of Experimental Psychology: Human, Perception and Performance, 14*, 693-706.

McClelland, J.L. (1979). On the time relations of mental processes: An examination of sytems of processes in cascade. *Psychological Review, 86*, 287-330.

McClelland, J.L. (1987). The case for interactionism in language processing. In M. Coltheart (Ed.), *Attention and performance, XII*. London: Lawrence Erlbaum Associates Limited.

McClelland, J.L. & Elman, J.L. (1986). The TRACE model of speech perception. *Cognitive Psychology, 18*, 1-86.

McClelland, J.L. & Rumelhart, D.E. (1981). An interactive activation model of context effects in letter perception: Part 1. An account of basic findings. *Psychological Review, 88*, 375-407.

McGuigan, F.J. (1970). Covert oral behavior during the silent performance of language tasks. *Psychological Bulletin, 74*, 309-326.

Meyer, D.E. & Schvaneveldt, R.W. (1971). Facilitation in recognizing pairs of words: Evidence of a dependence between retrieval operations. *Journal of Experimental Psychology, 90*, 227-234.

Meyer, D.E., Schvaneveldt, R.W., & Ruddy, M.G. (1974). Functions of graphemic and phonemic codes in visual word recognition. *Memory & Cognition, 2,* 309-321.

Mitchell, D.C. (1982). *The process of reading.* Chichester: John Wiley.

Mitchell, D.C. & Green, D.W. (1978). The effects of context and content on immediate processing in reading. *Quarterly Journal of Experimental Psychology, 30,* 609-636.

Mitchell, D.C., Sharkey, N.E., & Fox, J. (1983). *Search and evidence-collection models of lexical access: problems for both approaches.* Paper presented at the 10th Experimental Psychology Conference, University of Tasmania, Australia, 20–22 May.

Monsell, S. (1985). Repetition and the lexicon. In A.W. Ellis (Ed.), *Progress in the psychology of language, Vol. 2.* London: Lawrence Erlbaum Associates Limited.

Monsell, S., Doyle, M.C., & Haggard, P.N. (1989). Effects of frequency on word recognition tasks: Where are they? *Journal of Experimental Psychology: General, 118,* 43-71.

Morton, J. (1964). The effects of context on visual duration thresholds for words. *British Journal of Psychology, 55,* 165-180.

Morton, J. (1969). Interaction of information in word recognition. *Psychological Review, 76,* 165-178.

Morton, J. (1970). A functional model for memory. In D.A. Norman (Ed.), *Models of human memory.* New York: Academic Press.

Morton, J. (1979). Facilitation in word recognition: Experiments causing change in the logogen model. In P.A. Kolers, M. Wrolstad, & H. Bouma (Eds.), *Processing of visible language, Vol. 1.* New York: Plenum.

Morton, J. (1982). Disintegrating the lexicon: An information processing approach. In J. Mehler, E.C.T. Walker, & M. Garrett (Eds.), *Perspectives on mental representation.* Hillsdale, N.J.: Lawrence Erlbaum Associates Inc.

Murrell, G.A. & Morton, J. (1974). Word recognition and morphemic structure. *Journal of Experimental Psychology, 102,* 963-968.

Navon, D. & Shimron, J. (1981). Does word naming involve grapheme-to-phoneme translation? Evidence from Hebrew. *Journal of Verbal Learning and Verbal Behavior, 20,* 97-109.

Neely, J.H. (1976). Semantic priming and retrieval from lexical memory: evidence for facilitatory and inhibitory processes. *Memory & Cognition, 4,* 648-654.

Neely, J.H. (1977). Semantic priming and retrieval from lexical memory: roles of inhibitionless spreading activation and limited-capacity attention. *Journal of Experimental Psychology: General, 106,* 226-254.

Norris, D. (1986). Word recognition: Context effects without priming. *Cognition, 22,* 93-136.

Novik, N. (1974). Parallel processing in a word-nonword classification task. *Journal of Experimental Psychology, 102,* 1015-1020.

O'Connor, R.E. & Forster, K.I. (1981). Criterion bias and search sequence bias in word recognition. *Memory & Cognition, 9,* 78-92.

Oden, G.L. & Spira, J.L. (1983). Influence of context on the activation and selection of ambiguous word senses. *Quarterly Journal of Experimental Psychology, 35A,* 51-64.

O'Neil, W.M. (1953). The effect of verbal association on tachistoscopic recognition. *Australian Journal of Psychology, 5,* 42-45.

Onifer, W. & Swinney, D.A. (1981). Accessing lexical ambiguities during sentence comprehension: Effects of frequency of meaning and contextual bias. *Memory & Cognition, 9,* 225-236.

Paap, K.R., Newsome, S.L., McDonald, J.E., & Schvaneveldt, R.W. (1982). An activation-verification model for letter and word recognition. *Psychological Review, 89,* 573-594.

Paap, K.R., McDonald, J.E., Schvaneveldt, R.W., & Noel, R.W. (1987). Frequency and pronounceability in visually presented naming and lexical decision tasks. In M. Coltheart (Ed.), *Attention and performance, XII.* London: Lawrence Erlbaum Associates Limited.

Paivio, A. (1971). *Imagery and verbal processes.* New York: Holt, Rinehart, & Winston.

Paivio, A., Yuille, J.C., & Madigan, S.A. (1968). Concreteness, imagery and meaningfulness values for 925 nouns. *Journal of Experimental Psychology Monograph Supplement, 76* (1, Pt. 2).

Parkin, A.J. (1982). Phonological recoding in lexical decision: Effects of spelling-to-sound regularity depends upon how regularity is defined. *Memory & Cognition, 10,* 43-53.

Parkin, A.J. (1984). Redefining the regularity effect. *Memory & Cognition, 12,* 287-292.

Patterson, K.E. & Coltheart, V. (1987). Phonological processes in reading: A tutorial review. In M. Coltheart (Ed.), *Attention and performance, XII.* London: Lawrence Erlbaum Associates Limited.

Patterson, K.E. & Marcel, A.J. (1977). Aphasia, dyslexia and the phonological coding of written words. *Quarterly Journal of Experimental Psychology, 29,* 307-318.

Patterson, K.E., Marshall, J.C., & Coltheart, M. (1985). *Surface dyslexia.* London: Lawrence Erlbaum Associates Limited.

Patterson, K.E. & Morton, J. (1985). From orthography to phonology: An attempt at an old interpretation. In K.E. Patterson, J.C. Marshall, & M. Coltheart (Eds.), *Surface dyslexia.* London: Lawrence Erlbaum Associates Limited.

Perfetti, C.A., Bell, L.C., & Delaney, S.M. (1988). Automatic (prelexical) phonetic activation in silent word reading: Evidence from backward masking. *Journal of Memory and Language, 27,* 59-70.

Petocz, A. & Oliphant, G. (1988). Closed class words as first syllables do interfere with lexical decisions to nonwords—implications for theories of agrammatism. *Brain and Language, 34,* 127-146.

Posner, M.I. & Snyder, C.R.R. (1975) Attention and cognitive control. In R.L. Solso (Ed.), *Information processing and cognition: The Loyola Symposium.* Hillsdale, N.J.: Lawrence Erlbaum Associates Inc.

Prinzmetal, W., Treiman, R., & Rho, S.H. (1986). How to see a reading unit. *Journal of Memory and Language, 25,* 461-475.

Ratcliff, R. & McKoon, G. (1988). A retrieval theory of priming in memory. *Psychological Review, 95,* 385-408.

Rayner, K. (1983). *Eye movements in reading: Perceptual and language processes.* New York: Academic Press.

Rayner, K. (1989). *The psychology of reading.* Englewood Cliffs, N.J.: Prentice Hall.

Rayner, K. & Duffy, S.A. (1986). Lexical complexity and fixation times in reading: Effects of word frequency, verb complexity, and lexical ambiguity. *Memory & Cognition, 14*, 191-201.

Rosenberg, B., Zurif, E., Brownell, H., Garrett, M., & Bradley, D. (1985). Grammatical class effects in relation to normal and aphasic sentence processing. *Brain and Language, 26*, 287-303.

Rosson, M.B. (1983). From SOFA to LOUCH: Lexical contributions to pseudoword pronunciation. *Memory & Cognition, 11*, 152-160.

Rubenstein, H., Garfield, L., & Millikan, J.A. (1970). Homographic entries in the internal lexicon. *Journal of Verbal Learning and Verbal Behavior, 9*, 487-494.

Rubenstein, H., Lewis, S.S., & Rubenstein, M.A. (1971a). Evidence for phonemic recoding in visual word recognition. *Journal of Verbal Learning and Verbal Behavior, 10*, 645-657.

Rubenstein, H., Lewis, S.S., & Rubenstein, M.A. (1971b). Homographic entries in the internal lexicon: Effects of systematicity and relative frequency of meanings. *Journal of Verbal Learning and Verbal Behavior, 10*, 57-62.

Rubin, G.S., Becker, C.A., & Freeman, R.H. (1979). Morphological structure and its effect on visual word recognition. *Journal of Verbal Learning and Verbal Behavior, 18*, 757-767.

Rumelhart, D.E. & McClelland, J.L. (1982). An interactive activation model of context effects in letter perception: Part 2. *Psychological Review, 89*, 60-94.

Rumelhart, D.E., & McClelland, J.L. (1986). On learning the past tenses of English verbs. In J.L. McClelland, & D.E. Rumelhart (Eds.), *Parallel distributed processing: Explorations in the microstructure of cognition*. Cambridge, Mass.: MIT Press.

Savage, G.R., Bradley, D.C., & Forster, K.I. (1990). Word frequency and the pronunciation task: The contribution of articulatory fluency. *Language and Cognitive Processes, 5*, 203-236.

Scarborough, D.L., Cortese, C., & Scarborough H.S. (1977). Frequency and repetition effects in lexical memory. *Journal of Experimental Psychology: Human Perception and Performance, 3*, 1-17.

Schuberth, R. E. & Eimas, P. D. (1977). Effects of context on the classification of words and nonwords. *Journal of Experimental Psychology: Human Perception and Performance, 3*, 27-36.

Schuberth, R. E., Spoehr, K. T., & Lane, D. M. (1981). Effects of stimulus and contextual information on the lexical decision task. *Memory & Cognition, 9*, 68-77.

Schvaneveldt, R.W., Meyer, D.E., & Becker, C.A. (1976). Lexical ambiguity, semantic context and visual word recognition. *Journal of Experimental Psychology: Human Perception and Performance, 2*, 243-256.

Schwanenflugel, P.J. & Shoben, E.J. (1983). Differential context effects in the comprehension of abstract and concrete verbal materials. *Journal of Experimental Psychology: Learning, Memory, and Cognition, 9*, 82-102.

Segui, J. & Zubizarreta, M-L. (1985). Mental representation of morphologically complex words and lexical access. *Linguistics, 23*, 759-774.

Segui, J., Mehler, J., Frauenfelder, U., & Morton, J. (1982). The word frequency effect and lexical access. *Neuropsychologia, 20*, 615-627.

Seidenberg, M.S. (1985). The time course of phonological code activation in two writing systems. *Cognition, 19*, 1-30.

Seidenberg, M.S. (1987). Sublexical structures in visual word recognition: Access units or orthographic redundancy? In M. Coltheart (Ed.), *Attention and performance, XII*. London: Lawrence Erlbaum Associates Limited.

Seidenberg, M.S. (1989). Visual word recognition and pronunciation: A computational model and its implications. In W. Marslen-Wilson (Ed.), *Lexical representation and process*. Cambridge, Mass.: MIT Press.

Seidenberg, M.S. & McClelland, J.L. (1989). A distributed, developmental model of word recognition and naming. *Psychological Review, 96*, 523-568.

Seidenberg, M.S. & McClelland, J.L. (1990). More words but still no lexicon: Reply to Besner et al. (1990). *Psychological Review, 97*, 447-452.

Seidenberg, M.S., Tanenhaus, M.K., Leiman, J.M., & Bienkowski, M. (1982). Automatic access of the meanings of ambiguous words in context: Some limitations of knowledge-based processing. *Cognitive Psychology, 14*, 489-537.

Seidenberg, M.S., Waters, G.S., Sanders, M., & Langer, P. (1984a). Pre- and postlexical loci of contextual effects on word recognition. *Memory & Cognition, 12*, 315-328.

Seidenberg, M.S., Waters, G.S., Barnes, M.A., & Tanenhaus, M.K. (1984b). When does irregular spelling or pronunciation influence word recognition? *Journal of Verbal Learning and Verbal Behavior, 23*, 383-404.

Selkirk, E. (1982). *The syntax of words*. Cambridge, Mass.: MIT Press.

Shallice, T. & McCarthy, R. (1985). Phonological reading: From patterns of impairment to possible procedures. In K.E. Patterson, J.C. Marshall, & M. Coltheart (Eds.), *Surface dyslexia*. London: Lawrence Erlbaum Associates Limited.

Shallice, T., Warrington, E.K., & McCarthy, R. (1983). Reading without semantics. *Quarterly Journal of Experimental Psychology, 35A*, 111-138.

Shapiro, L.P. & Jensen, L.R. (1986). Processing open and closed class-headed nonwords: Left hemisphere support for separate vocabularies. *Brain and Language, 28*, 318-327.

Shulman, H., Hornak, R., & Sanders, E. (1978). The effects of graphemic, phonemic, and semantic relationships on access to lexical structures. *Memory & Cognition, 6*, 115-123.

Simpson, G.B. (1981). Meaning dominance and semantic context in the processing of lexical ambiguity. *Journal of Verbal Learning and Verbal Behavior, 20*, 120-136.

Simpson, G.B., Peterson, R.R., Casteel, M.A., & Burgess, C. (1989). Lexical and sentence context effects in word recognition. *Journal of Experimental Psychology: Learning, Memory, and Cognition, 15*, 88-97.

Smith, P.T. & Sterling, C.M. (1982). Factors affecting the perceived morphemic structure of written words. *Journal of Verbal Learning and Verbal Behavior, 21*, 704-721.

Spoehr, K.T. & Smith, E.E. (1973). The role of syllables in perceptual processing. *Cognitive Psychology, 5*, 71-89.

Stanhope N. & Parkin, A.J. (1987). Further explorations of the consistency effect in word and nonword pronunciation. *Memory & Cognition, 15*, 169-179.

Stanners, R.F. & Forbach, G.B. (1973). Analysis of letter strings in word recognition. *Journal of Experimental Psychology, 98*, 31-35.

Stanners, R.F., Forbach, G.B., & Headley, D.B. (1971). Decision and search processes in word-nonword classification. *Journal of Experimental Psychology, 90*, 45-50.

Stanners, R.F., Jastrzembski, J.E., & Westbrook, A. (1975). Frequency and visual quality in a word-nonword classification task. *Journal of Verbal Learning and Verbal Behavior, 14*, 259-264.

Stanners, R.F., Neiser, J.J., & Painton, S. (1979a). Memory representations for prefixed words. *Journal of Verbal Learning and Verbal Behavior, 18*, 733-743.

Stanners, R.F., Neiser, J.J., Hernon, W.P., & Hall, R. (1979b). Memory representation for morphologically related words. *Journal of Verbal Learning and Verbal Behavior, 18*, 399-412.

Stanovich, K. E. (1980). Toward an interactive-compensatory model of individual differences in the development of reading fluency. *Reading Research Quarterly, 16*, 32-71.

Stanovich, K. E. (1981).Attentional and automatic context effects in reading. In A. M. Lesgold & C. A. Perfetti (Eds.), *Interactive processes in reading*. Hillsdale, N.J.: Lawrence Erlbaum Associates Inc.

Stanovich, K. E. & Bauer, D.W. (1978). Experiments on the spelling-to-sound regularity effect in word recognition. *Memory & Cognition, 6*, 410-415.

Stanovich, K. E. & West, R. F. (1979). Mechanisms of sentence context effects in reading: Automatic activation and conscious attention. *Memory & Cognition, 7*, 77-85.

Stanovich, K. E. & West, R. F. (1981). The effect of sentence context on ongoing word recognition: Tests of a two-process theory. *Journal of Experimental Psychology: Human Perception and Performance, 7*, 638-678.

Stanovich, K. E. & West, R. F. (1983). On priming by a sentence context. *Journal of Experimental Psychology: General, 112*, 1-36.

Stetson, R.H. (1951). *Motor phonetics: A study of speech movements in action.* Amsterdam: North Holland.

Swinney, D.A. (1979). Lexical access during sentence comprehension: (Re)consideration of context effects. *Journal of Verbal Learning and Verbal Behavior, 18*, 645-659.

Swinney, D.A., Zurif, E.B., & Cutler, A. (1980). Effects of sentential stress and word class upon comprehension of Broca's aphasia. *Brain and Language, 10*, 132-144.

Tabossi, P. (1988). Accessing lexical ambiguity in different types of sentential contexts. *Journal of Memory and Language, 27*, 324-340.

Taft, M. (1979a). Recognition of affixed words and the word frequency effect. *Memory & Cognition, 7*, 263-272.

Taft, M. (1979b). Lexical access via an orthographic code: The Basic Orthographic Syllabic Structure (BOSS). *Journal of Verbal Learning and Verbal Behavior, 18*, 21-39.

Taft, M. (1981). Prefix stripping revisited. *Journal of Verbal Learning and Verbal Behavior, 20*, 289-297.

Taft, M. (1982). An alternative to grapheme-phoneme conversion rules? *Memory & Cognition, 10*, 465-474

Taft, M. (1984). Evidence for an abstract lexical representation of word structure. *Memory & Cognition, 12*, 264-269.

Taft, M. (1985). The decoding of words in lexical access: A review of the morphographic approach. In D. Besner, T.G. Waller, & G.E. MacKinnon (Eds.), *Reading research: Advances in theory and practice, Vol. V*. Academic Press, New York.

Taft, M. (1986). Lexical access codes in visual and auditory word recognition. *Language & Cognitive Processes, 1*, 49-60.

Taft, M. (1987). Morphographic processing. The BOSS re-emerges. In M. Coltheart (Ed.), *Attention and performance, XII*. London: Lawrence Erlbaum Associates Limited.

Taft, M. (1990). Lexical processing of functionally constrained words. *Journal of Memory and Language, 29*, 245-257.

Taft, M. & Cottrell, D. (1988). *On converting print to sound and sound to print*. Paper presented at the 24th International Congress of Psychology, Sydney, Australia, August.

Taft, M. & Forster, K.I. (1975). Lexical storage and retrieval of prefixed words. *Journal of Verbal Learning and Verbal Behavior, 14*, 638-647.

Taft, M. & Forster, K.I. (1976). Lexical storage and retrieval of polymorphemic and polysyllabic words. *Journal of Verbal Learning and Verbal Behavior, 15*, 607-620.

Taft, M. & Hambly, G. (1985). The influence of orthography on phonological representations in the lexicon. *Journal of Memory & Language, 24*, 320-335.

Taft, M., Hambly, G., & Kinoshita, S. (1986). Visual and auditory recognition of prefixed words. *Quarterly Journal of Experimental Psychology: Human Experimental Psychology, 38A*, 351-366

Tanenhaus, M.K., Leiman, J.M., & Seidenberg, M.S. (1979). Evidence for multiple stages in the processing of ambiguous words in syntactic contexts. *Journal of Verbal Learning and Verbal Behavior, 18*, 427-440.

Taraban, R. & McClelland, J.L. (1987). Conspiracy effects in word pronunciation. *Journal of Memory and Language, 26*, 608-631.

Taylor, G.A., Miller, T.J., & Juola, J.F. (1977). Isolating visual units in the perception of words and nonwords. *Perception & Psychophysics, 21*, 377-386.

Treiman, R. & Chafetz, J. (1987). Are there onset- and rime-like units in printed words. In M. Coltheart (Ed.), *Attention and performance, XII*. London: Lawrence Erlbaum Associates Limited.

Treiman, R. & Zukowski, A. (1988). Units in reading and spelling. *Journal of Memory and Language, 27*, 466-477.

Treiman, R., Freyd, J.J., & Baron, J. (1983). Phonological recoding and use of spelling-sound rules in reading sentences. *Journal of Verbal Learning and Verbal Behavior, 22*, 682-700.

Treiman, R., Goswami, U., & Bruck, M. (1990). Not all nonwords are alike: Implications for reading development and theory. *Memory & Cognition, 18*, 559-567.

Tulving, E. (1972). Episodic and semantic memory. In E. Tulving & W. Donaldson (Eds.), *Organization of memory*. New York: Academic Press.

Tulving, E & Gold C. (1963). Stimulus information and contextual information as determinants of tachistoscopic recognition of words. *Journal of Experimental Psychology, 66*, 319-327.

Tweedy, J.R. & Lapinski, R.H. (1981). Facilitating word recognition: evidence for strategic and automatic factors. *Quarterly Journal of Experimental Psychology, 33A*, 51-60.

Tweedy, J.R., Lapinski, R.H., & Schvaneveldt, R.W. (1981). Semantic context effects on word recognition: influence of varying the proportion of items presented in an appropriate context. *Memory & Cognition, 5*, 84-89.

Underwood, G., Roberts, M., & Thomason, H. (1988). Strategical invariance in lexical access: The reappearance of the pseudohomophone effect. *Canadian Journal of Psychology, 42*, 24-34.

Underwood, G., Hubbard, A., & Wilkinson, H. (1990). Eye fixations predict reading comprehension: The relationship between reading skill, reading speed, and visual inspection. *Language and Speech, 33*, 69-81.

Van Orden, G.C. (1987). A ROWS is a ROSE: Spelling, sound, and reading. *Memory & Cognition, 15*, 181-198.

Van Orden, G.C., Johnston, J.C., & Hale, B. L. (1988). Word identification in reading proceeds from spelling to sound to meaning. *Journal of Experimental Psychology: Learning, Memory, and Cognition, 14*, 371-386.

Venezky, R. (1970). *The structure of English orthography*. The Hague: Mouton

Warren, C.E.J. & Morton, J. (1982). The effects of priming on picture recognition. *British Journal of Psychology, 73*, 117-130.

Waters, G.S. & Seidenberg, M.S. (1985). Spelling-sound effects in reading: Time course and decision criteria. *Memory & Cognition, 13*, 557-572.

West, R.F. & Stanovich, K.E. (1978). Automatic contextual facilitation in readers of three ages. *Child Development, 49*, 717-727.

West, R.F. & Stanovich, K.E. (1982). Source of inhibition in experiments on the effect of sentence context on word recognition. *Journal of Experimental Psychology: Learning, Memory, and Cognition, 8*, 385-399.

West, R.F. & Stanovich, K.E. (1986). Robust effects of syntactic structure on visual word processing. *Memory & Cognition, 14*, 104-112.

Whaley, C.P. (1978). Word-nonword classification time. *Journal of Verbal Learning and Verbal Behavior, 17*, 143-154.

Wickelgren, W.A. (1969). Context-sensitive coding, associative memory, and serial order in (speech) behavior. *Psychological Review, 76*, 1-15.

Winnick, W.A. & Daniel, S.A. (1970). Two kinds of response priming in tachistoscopic recognition. *Journal of Experimental Psychology, 84*, 74-81.

Wright, B. & Garrett, M. (1984). Lexical decision in sentences: Effects of syntactic structure. *Memory & Cognition, 12*, 31-45.

Author Index

Subject Index

Titles in the Series
Essays in Cognitive Psychology
Series Editors: Alan Baddeley, Max Coltheart, Leslie Henderson & Phil Johnson-Laird

IMPLICIT LEARNING
Theoretical and Empirical Issues

DIANNE C. BERRY (University of Reading),
ZOLTAN DIENES (University of Sussex)

There is considerable debate over the extent to which cognitive tasks can be learned non-consciously or implicitly. In recent years a large number of studies have demonstrated a discrepancy between explicit knowledge and measured performance. This book presents an overview of these studies and attempts to clarify apparently disparate results by placing them in a coherent theoretical framework.

It draws on evidence from neuropsychological and computational modelling studies as well as the many laboratory experiments.

Chapter one sets out the background to the large number of recent studies on implicit learning. It discusses research on implicit memory, perception without awareness, and automaticity. It attempts to set the implicit - explicit distinction in the context of other relevant dichotomies in the literature. Chapter two presents an overview of research on the control of complex systems, from Broadbent (1977) through to the present day. It looks at the accessibility of control task knowledge, as well as whether there is any other evidence for a distinction between implicit and explicit modes of learning. Chapter three critically reviews studies claiming to show that people can acquire concepts without being verbally aware of the basis on which they are responding. It shows that concept formation can be implicit in some sense but not in others. Chapter four investigates the claim that people can learn sequential information in an implicit way. Chapter five looks at whether computational modelling can elucidate the nature of implicit learning. It examines the feasibility of different exemplar connectionist models in accounting for performance in concept learning, sequence learning, and control task experiments. Chapter six reviews evidence concerning dissociations between implicit and explicit knowledge in various neuropsychological syndromes. Finally, chapters seven and eight discuss the many practical and theoretical implications of the research.

Contents: Preface. Towards a Characterisation of Implicit Learning. The Control of Complex Systems. Implicit Concept Formation. Sequence Learning. Computational Models of Implicit Learning. Neuropsychological Evidence. Practical Implications. Theoretical Implications. *References.*

ISBN 0-86377-223-4 1993 208pp. $37.50 £19.95 hbk

For UK/Europe, please send orders to: Lawrence Erlbaum Associates Ltd., Mail Order Department, 27 Church Road, Hove, East Sussex, BN3 2FA, England. Note, prices shown here are correct at time of going to press, but may change. Prices outside Europe may differ from those shown. Please send USA & Canadian orders to: Lawrence Erlbaum Associates Inc., 365 Broadway, Hillsdale, New Jersey, NJ07642, USA.

Titles in the Series
Essays in Cognitive Psychology
Series Editors: Alan Baddeley, Max Coltheart, Leslie Henderson & Phil Johnson-Laird

COMMUNICATING QUANTITIES
A Psychological Perspective
LINDA M. MOXEY, ANTHONY J. SANFORD
(University of Glasgow)

Every day, in many situations, we use expressions which seem only vaguely to provide us with information. The weather forecaster tells us that "some showers are likely in Northern regions during the night", a statement which is vague with respect to number of showers, location, and time. Yet such messages are informative, and often it is not possible for the producer of the message to be more precise. A tutor tells his students that "only a few students fail their exams outright". This does not give a precise incidence. Yet it might be equally misleading to do so. For example, to say that 12% failed outright last year says nothing about other years, while to say an average of 8% over the last five years says nothing about variability. We argue that a precise, numerical statement can be sometimes more misleading in reality than a vague statement.

Many researchers in psychology have attempted to capture the meaning of quantities by relating them to scales of quantity. The book explores this idea in detail and shows with original studies how these expressions also serve to control attention and to convey information about the expectations held by those involved in the communication.

The book works towards a psychological theory of the meaning of quantifiers and similarly vague terms. New links are drawn between formal theories of quantification and psychological experimentation.

Contents: Introduction. Quantifiers and Quantities. Scales and Negatives. Focus and Attention Control. Focus: Foundations and Extensions. Further Aspects of Inference. Towards a Psychological Account of Quantifiers. *References. Author Index. Subject Index.*

ISBN 0-86377-225-0 1993 144pp. $37.50 £19.95 hbk

For UK/Europe, please send orders to: Lawrence Erlbaum Associates Ltd., Mail Order Department, 27 Church Road, Hove, East Sussex, BN3 2FA, England. Note, prices shown here are correct at time of going to press, but may change. Prices outside Europe may differ from those shown. Please send USA & Canadian orders to: Lawrence Erlbaum Associates Inc., 365 Broadway, Hillsdale, New Jersey, NJ07642, USA.